You live in a world that is filled with surprises. Did you know that there are *three* North Poles? That a new kind of airplane flies on sun power alone? That swarming bees almost never sting? That a specially designed tricycle can travel faster than the U. S. speed limit? That dogs and cats love garlic? That some creatures "play dead" for years and then come back to life? That a whale shark can weigh as much as 11 large cars? When you finish reading this book, you'll be able to amaze your friends with these and many other far-out facts.

My, what big eyes you have! Sharp eyes that look like goggles help the net-casting spider catch its dinner. The small Australian spider weaves a net, then waits for insects to come within striking range. When the spider spots an insect, it stretches the net between its legs. Then it leaps and catches the insect in the net. The net-casting spider needs good eyesight for another reason. It does its hunting by night.

MANTIS WILDLIFE FILMS/OXFORD SCIENTIFIC FILMS

more
FAR-OUT
FACTS

■ BOOKS FOR WORLD EXPLORERS
NATIONAL GEOGRAPHIC SOCIETY

Contents

This lightweight airplane, called the Solar Challenger (above), flies on sun power alone. Read more about this unusual plane on pages 98 through 101.

RANDA BISHOP/CONTACT

COVER: *Without leaving the ground, a test pilot learns what it would be like to travel at more than twice the speed of sound. The pilot sits in a model cockpit that rests on a large metal arm. The arm raises, lowers, and tilts the cockpit. Colored lights on the cockpit trace its motions for the camera. All the motions are computer controlled. Computers often help engineers design and test aircraft. You'll see some of these aircraft on pages 10 through 14 and discover other uses for computers on pages 50 through 54.*

JAMES A. SUGAR (COVER)

Animals Far From Home

Elephants in snowy Canada? Polar bears in Washington, D. C.? These animals live far from their natural homes. They are adjusting to new homes in zoos and wildlife parks.

People who run the zoos and parks help the animals adjust. They study the animals' needs and try to meet them. Elephants, for example, normally live in warm places. To survive in a cold climate, they need shelter and extra food. Polar bears live in a cold climate. In warm areas, such as Washington, D. C., they need pools where they can cool off on hot summer days.

Keepers try to feed animals foods similar to those they would eat in the wild. They add vitamins and minerals to ensure that the animals will get everything they need.

Animals in zoos and parks take up new activities. Freed from the need to search for food, many animals play games and learn tricks. Some, such as elephants and dolphins, perform in shows. The activities seem to keep them healthier and happier than animals with nothing to do.

These three elephants were born in Africa. There they never walked in snow. Now the elephants live in Ontario, in Canada. Their home is a wild-game park called African Lion Safari. Winters in Ontario are cold and snowy. The small amount of hair on the hides of elephants provides no warmth. Caretakers help the huge creatures adapt to the colder climate. They feed the animals a richer diet during the winter, which helps them keep warm. They also keep the animals in a heated barn on cold days. The elephants don't spend all winter in the barn, however. Every day they exercise outdoors for short periods. In the wild, elephants are active, spending most of their time searching for food and eating. Short periods outdoors, even in winter, help elephants in the park get the exercise they need to stay healthy.

SUE BRADNAM

Is that a striped lion, or are those unstriped tigers (below)? The answer is neither. These two kinds of cats grew up in the same enclosure at African Lion Safari, in Canada. In the wild, lions and tigers would never meet. Tigers live only in Asia, and lions live mostly in Africa. Normally neither kind of wild cat would allow another kind of cat near it. Yet these animals lived together peacefully for three years. The tiger changed some of its habits. In the wild, tigers usually live alone. Lions live in family groups. This tiger joined a lion group. It became active by day, as lions are. Wild tigers are active mostly by night.

ANIMALS ANIMALS/DAN BALIOTTI

Two cheetahs (right) rest in front of a chateau, or castle, in France. France? Yes, this is Chateau Thoiry (sha-TOE twa-REE). The grounds of the chateau, near Paris, are filled with game. Wild animals from around the world live in huge gardens and open fields surrounding the chateau. The cheetahs are far from their African homeland. Like many of the other animals, the cheetahs had to adapt, or change, to survive in a foreign place. French winters are colder than winters in the parts of Africa where most cheetahs live. The cheetahs' spotted coats grew unusually thick in the winter. Although wild cheetahs avoid people, those at the chateau became used to large crowds of visitors. These particular cheetahs, with collars, had been pets. The owners gave them to the park, where caretakers released them with other cheetahs.

Busy Bees

The old woman in the shoe could have learned something about organization from a queen honeybee. The queen has a family of thousands! Her family builds its own wax home in a hollow tree or in stacked boxes provided by a beekeeper. A beehive is about the size of a small doghouse. In summer, the hive may be home to as many as 60,000 bees. Each hive has only one queen, and she has only one job—to lay about 1,500 eggs a day. Worker bees do all the household chores and bring in all the food. The youngest workers stay inside the hive. They clean the wax cells, care for the eggs, and feed the wormlike hatchlings, called larvae (LAR-vee). After about three weeks, workers graduate to jobs outside. They fly to flowers, where they gather pollen and nectar, the sweet liquid bees make into honey. Workers usually stay within a mile and a half of the hive (2 km).* They make as many as 50 trips a day. In about six weeks, they wear out their wings and die. But during their short lives, bees do some amazing things.

*Metric figures in this book have been rounded off.

If a hive becomes too crowded, the bees produce a second queen. Soon after this, the old queen flies away. About 30,000 workers—half the bees in the hive—go with her. They form a large group called a swarm. Most of the swarm settles on a tree (above), a fence, or any handy object, while a few dozen bees look for a new place to live. Swarming bees have no hive to defend, so they do not sting unless they are roughly handled. Beekeeper Marc Caputo, of Fredericksburg, Ohio, shows his bee "beard" to his children, Kacey, 7, and Toby, 3. Caputo attracted the bees by hanging a caged queen bee around his neck. When he removes the caged queen, his "beard" will follow her.

MARC M. CAPUTO

When it's cold outside, bees form a living furnace in the hive. Anytime the temperature falls below 57°F (14°C), workers gather in big balls on the sides of the honeycombs and "dance" (left). The bees wriggle their bodies, stamp their feet, tug at each other, and rotate their wings. These movements produce enough heat to keep the bees warm. As the weather becomes colder, the bees draw together more tightly. Their movements speed up. Tired bees crawl to the outer layer of the ball for a rest. Others crawl into the center and replace them.

During a heat wave, bees provide their own air conditioning. Without it, the larvae would die. Workers fly to streams and puddles and fill their stomachs with water. Mouth to mouth, they pass the water to workers in the nursery. The nursery workers use their tongues to spread water on the lids of cells that hold larvae (left). These workers constantly fan their wings to stir up a breeze. The breeze makes the water evaporate quickly, cooling the cells.

Have you ever heard people say they could smell trouble? Bees really can. If an enemy—or any large creature—appears at the hive entrance, the bees there quickly warn those inside. The guard bees face the enemy (right). They lift their stingers and extend them. This action triggers a scent gland near each stinger. The gland releases an alarm scent. The guards rotate their wings, driving air across their bodies and fanning the scent into the hive. To bees inside, this scent means "Danger! Help!" They rush out, ready to sting the enemy and defend the hive.

Each beehive has a special smell that its own bees recognize. When young bees first leave the hive to gather nectar or pollen, they may have trouble finding their way back. To guide the young bees home, others in their hive gather at the entrance (left). They release a scent from their bodies. The bees fan the scent into the air with their wings. Wandering bees detect it with their sensitive antennae, or feelers, and follow it home.

Long live the queen! And she does—for two or three years. During that time, she lays about a million eggs. Workers constantly attend her (right)—grooming, cleaning, and stroking her. The queen's body produces a milky fluid. Every day, workers pass a taste of it from one to another. The queen also has a special odor. This combination of taste and odor keeps the workers calm. When a queen dies, the workers immediately become very excited. They quickly feed a lot of a substance called royal jelly to a few larvae in queen cells. In 15 or 16 days, a new queen crawls out of one of the cells. She destroys the other queen cells. As soon as the new queen begins laying eggs, the hive settles down.

ROZ SCHANZER (ART)

Strange Planes

If someone asked you to tell what an airplane looks like and how it flies, you'd probably describe a bullet-shaped craft with one wing on each side. You might say that the plane taxis to a long runway. It gathers speed and takes off for a fast flight. You'd be right about most airplanes, but not all.

Some airplanes flying today don't fit that description. Some can take off without a runway. Others have a single wing. Some have propellers where other planes have tails.

A few aircraft look more like kites than planes. These planes, called ultralights, usually fly close to the ground. They cruise very slowly for a plane—at about the speed of a fast car.

A few airplanes have four wings instead of two. A pair of short wings near the nose of such a plane is called a canard (kuh-NARD). That's the French word for duck. Some people think the wings got this name because they make an airplane look like a duck in flight. In the early 1900s, the Wright brothers used canards on their flying machines. In the 1970s, a designer named Burt Rutan tried canards again. He discovered that the extra wings enable planes to use less fuel.

Many people who fly as a hobby build their own planes. Rutan's planes can be built at home from kits. You'll read more about these and other unusual aircraft on the next pages.

Like pincers on a giant insect, the rear wings of an aircraft called the Rutan Defiant seem to grip Soledad Mountain. The mountain rises from the Mojave Desert in California. Tilted wingtips called winglets help keep the aircraft steady as it flies. A camera mounted on the nose of the Defiant took this picture.

JAMES A. SUGAR

Three different Rutan aircraft make a triple-decker flight over the Mojave Desert. They are, from the top, a Long-EZ, a Vari-Viggen, and a VariEze. All three aircraft come in kit form. Do-it-yourselfers can build these airplanes at home. The airplanes at top and bottom are made of foam and fiberglass. The plane in the center is made mostly of wood.

Airplanes fly because their wings lift them upward on currents of air. As an engine pushes a plane forward, pressure decreases on the curved tops of its wings and increases under its wings. The buildup of pressure lifts the plane. This drawing (right) shows how the design of the VariEze adds to its lift. Air striking the tips of the canard spins and rises. The main wings pass through the rising air, which gives them more lift. The turned-up tips on the main wings are used in turning and controlling the plane. They take the place of the rudder usually found on an airplane's tail. The propeller is at the rear, so the plane doesn't have to move through churned-up air.

MARK SEIDLER AND SUSAN M. JOHNSTON, N.G.S.

A light aircraft called a Breezy circles over Fond du Lac, Wisconsin (below). Steel tubing forms the plane's body, and striped fabric covers one large wing. The aircraft has a top speed of 85 miles an hour (137 km/h). Here it cruises at 40 to 50 miles an hour (64 to 80 km/h). Pilot Lee Perrizo and photographer Jerry Irwin get a closeup view of fields and farms. They can even smell the smoke from barbecues! They don't wear parachutes since chutes would be useless this close to the ground. If the engine should fail, the pilot can glide the craft to a safe landing.

JERRY IRWIN

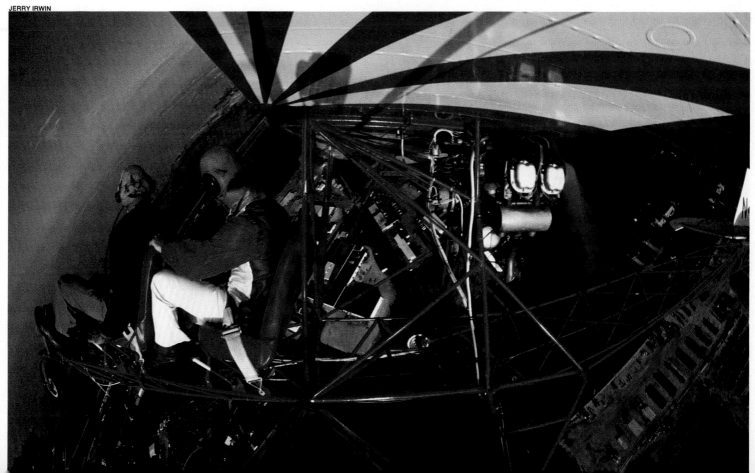

Swooping out of the night sky, a jet fighter
makes a vertical landing. This U. S. Marine
Corps airplane is called a Harrier. British
engineers who designed the Harrier named it
after a sleek, swift marsh hawk. Special lights
and camera equipment show the path the
plane takes as it comes down. This jet doesn't
need a long runway. It can take off or land in a
space the size of a tennis court! In the air, the
Harrier can change position quickly. It can
turn sharply and make steep, fast dives. The
pilot turns four nozzles on the plane to
change the direction of the thrust, or push,
from the engines. When the nozzles point
straight down, the plane moves straight up.
When they point toward the rear of the plane,
the Harrier flies forward.

JAMES A. SUGAR

Tunnel Vision

You're riding the New York City subway from Brooklyn to Manhattan and looking out the window. Suddenly you see colorful shapes. They move, change, and dissolve. A bright red ball becomes a machine . . . a plant . . . a human . . . and a rocket that blasts off! It's all over in 20 seconds. But what is it?

It's Masstransiscope (mass-TRAN-zih-scope), according to Bill Brand, the filmmaker who created it. He made up the word to describe this underground animated movie. The subway is a form of mass transit, or transportation. A scope is a viewing instrument.

Brand used a working model (left) to help him design his film. Drawings that show step-by-step action wind from one big spool to another. A strip of black paper with up-and-down slits in it spins around inside the box. To see his "movie," Brand peers through a window in the box and through the slits in the paper. As he watches the drawings through the slits, the figures seem to spring to life.

On the subway the process is reversed, but the effect is the same. "Usually the film moves, and the viewer sits still," Brand explains. "Here, the viewer moves and the film sits still."

Two hundred twenty-eight pictures line the back wall of a long box on an unused subway platform. The front wall of the box has narrow slits. As trains whiz by the box, the passengers see a lively show.

In the darkness of a subway tunnel (right), a train rolls by the Masstransiscope. Hundreds of fluorescent bulbs surround the slits in the box, lighting up the action. Brand grins as he watches people watching his animated movie. "I wanted to provide subway riders with the same kind of delight that viewers of the first motion pictures experienced," he says. Brand completed Masstransiscope in 1980. Since then, 10,000 people have seen it every day. What do they think of it? "It wakes me up in the morning," says one regular subway rider. "I always look forward to seeing it. I purposely sit on the side of the train that faces the art. It's like fantasy fireworks bursting out of the night sky."

MARTHA COOPER (BOTH)

Masked MINI-MONSTERS

On a twig in a tropical forest, a tiny egg hatches. The insect that crawls out doesn't look like anything special. It's a wingless, spiny blob. The blob pushes a needle-shaped mouth into the twig. Then it starts sucking plant juices. As it feeds and grows, it changes into . . .

. . . A MINI-MONSTER! A hard plate forms on the insect's back. Soon, the plate takes on a strange shape. It makes the insect look like a creature from space.

This mini-monster is called a treehopper. About 2,300 kinds of treehoppers live on weeds and trees all over the world. Those that live in cool climates have plain, hard shells covering their bodies. Those that live in hot climates grow strange-looking armor on their backs.

Scientists call a treehopper's backplate a pronotum (pro-NO-tum). You'll see some monstrous-looking backplates on these and the following pages. But don't worry. The treehoppers that own them are all less than an inch long.

Three oddly shaped bumps on a log (below)? No, you're looking at two bumps and one insect called a treehopper. This isn't actually a log. It's a small twig. Can you spot the treehopper? It's the "bump" in the middle. Legs and thin wings give it away. A hard plate on its back forms the strange, branching shape that looks like part of the twig. The backplate is called a pronotum (pro-NO-tum). Many treehoppers have backplates that grow into fantastic shapes. They make the insects look top-heavy. You'd think they wouldn't be able to fly, but they can—quite fast. They can also hop for short distances.

KJELL B. SANDVED/SMITHSONIAN INSTITUTION

Young treehoppers, called nymphs, line up at feeding stations on a plant stem (left). As soon as the young hatched, they made openings in the twig with their mouths. Then they began sucking plant juices. Some treehopper nymphs don't have to make the openings themselves. Their mothers do it for them — before the nymphs hatch.

A female treehopper guards a cluster of eggs (below). Treehopper eggs usually hatch in about 20 days. Many females lay their eggs and leave them, but some kinds care for the young. This kind of treehopper will make feeding slits for her nymphs. As they hatch, she will nudge them toward the slits. She will stay with them for about a month, guarding them against hungry spiders, ladybugs, and other enemies. She will also make the nymphs stay at their feeding stations.

PAUL A. ZAHL, PH.D. (ALL)

These treehoppers look as if they are carrying ants (left). The "ants" are actually the treehoppers' backplates. Scientists think that ant disguises may help protect treehoppers from enemies for one of these reasons: 1) Larger insects may avoid ants because they taste bad or because ants defend themselves by biting and stinging. 2) Ants defend smaller insects fiercely if the ants are using those insects as "cows." Ants stroke treehoppers and some other sap-sucking insects to make them ooze a sweet liquid that the ants drink. Ant-shaped backplates may attract real ants to the treehoppers.

DRAYTON HAWKINS, N.G.S. (ALL ART)

17

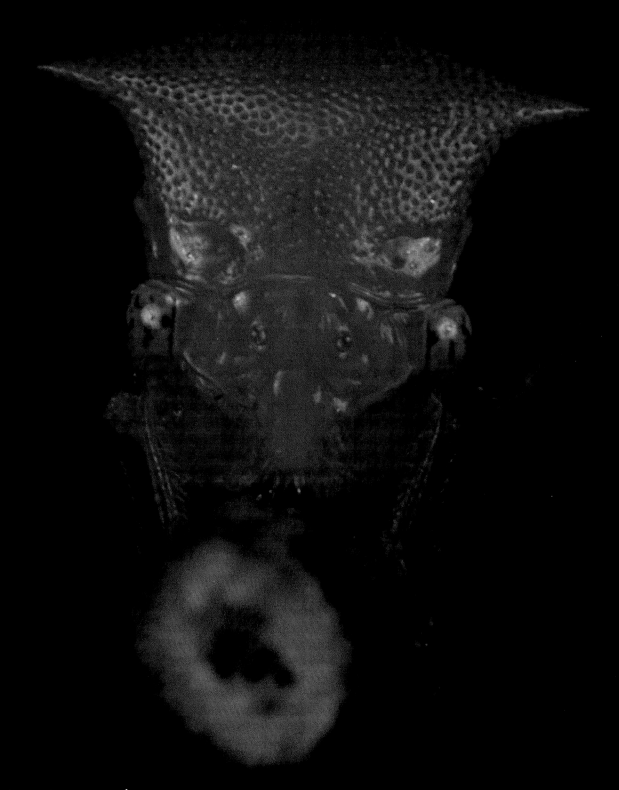

Sharp spikes on a hard pronotum may make this kind of treehopper hard to eat. Some scientists think the spikes scratch the throat of a bird or a lizard that tries to swallow the treehopper. What looks like a green spotlight in front of the treehopper is reflected light from the broken end of a twig.

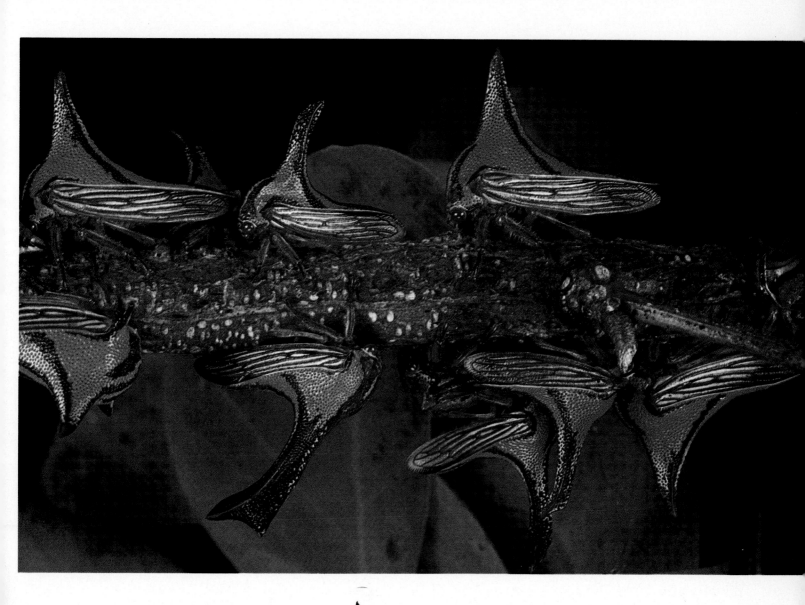

Does it look as if one of these thorns (above) grew in the wrong direction? That's not surprising. All of the "thorns" on this twig are really young adult treehoppers. At this stage, they have soft, colorful shields. Soon the shields will harden. Their colors will become darker. The treehoppers will leave the twig to mate and lay eggs. Some scientists think the shape of the pronotum helps males and females of the same kind recognize each other. These females have shields with sharp points that stick straight up. The shields of these males slant backward slightly and end in blunt tips. Can you count the males and females in this picture?

Perched on a pencil eraser, a treehopper doesn't look scary at all. This one, often called a thorn bug, grows no longer than $1/2$ inch (13 mm). A single treehopper can't suck enough juice from a plant to harm it. But large groups of treehoppers can cause twigs to wilt. Treehoppers often make whirring or buzzing noises with their wings. They do this at mating time, or when they are frightened or attacked. Sometimes the whirring wings of a treehopper can actually knock an attacker off a branch. The noises treehoppers make are so faint that most people never hear them.

DRAYTON HAWKINS (ART)

19

Far-out Contests

Who runs fastest? Who jumps highest? Who can lift the most weight? Who throws a ball farthest? Whose horse, car, boat, bicycle, or airplane reaches the highest speed? To find out, people take part in contests.

People have competed in contests throughout history. Citizens of ancient Greece held the Olympic games in honor of Zeus, king of their gods. In ancient Rome, children tested their strength in tug-of-war matches. Long before Columbus sailed to America, Central American Indians competed in ball games and foot races.

Although many of today's contests are serious tests of athletic ability, some are held primarily for fun. People race through the streets flipping pancakes. They bounce and slide down ski slopes on giant inner tubes. They get off the ground in homemade airplanes and hot-air balloons. They stage races with crabs, worms, turkeys, camels, and tortoises.

Sometimes it seems that people will race *anything* — even things that ordinarily don't move. On the next page, you'll see

Ready for a race, colorful balloons crowd the sky at the Balloon Fiesta. It's held every October, in Albuquerque, New Mexico, and it's the largest hot-air ballooning event in the world. A half million people watch hundreds of balloonists compete. Contests include a "roadrunner and coyote" race. The balloon that is the "roadrunner" takes off first. The "coyotes" try to catch it.

Steve McIntosh zips along in a super tricycle called the Vector (above). He's racing at the annual Human-Powered Speed Championships in Pomona, California. Huffy, a bicycle manufacturer, sponsored him. The bullet-shaped tricycle set a world record for one-person vehicles: 58.7 miles an hour (94 km/h). Designers gave the Vector three wheels instead of two to make it more stable. The lightweight body rolls along on narrow tires. But don't get any ideas about riding around in a Vector. This tricycle costs about $10,000. A rider has to use it on a smooth racing surface because its body lies only an inch (2^1/$_2$ cm) above the ground.

Another speedy Vector is a three-wheeled version of the bicycle built for two (right). Hugh Walton pedals and steers. Bruce Donaghy pedals with both his hands and his feet. Together, they can get the tricycle moving at 62.9 miles an hour (101 km/h). Both Vectors can travel faster than the U. S. speed limit for automobiles.

Rub-a-dub-dub. Sailors in bathtubs use outboard motors to chug across choppy water (below). They get a bumpy ride on the Strait of Georgia, off Vancouver Island, during the Great International Bathtub Race. The competition takes place every year in British Columbia, in Canada. Since 1967, sailors of all ages have built bathtub boats especially for this race. The contestants make lightweight fiberglass versions of old-fashioned bathtubs. They mount their tubs on water skis or on plywood bases and add motors. The rules of the race say that no entry can be more than 6 feet long (2 m) and 3 feet wide (1 m). Larger boats accompany the bathtubs in case of trouble. Helicopters hover overhead, ready to make quick rescues. Such safety precautions are necessary. In 1981, waves 8 to 10 feet high (2 to 3 m) towered over the bathtub racers. Many outboard motors stalled. Some boats broke apart in the pounding waves. Others sank. In fact, only 30 of the 133 competitors made it across the strait. The winner of the bathtub race completed the 36-mile (58-km) crossing in an hour and 19 minutes.

DAVID FALCONER

As far as the eye can see, camels fill the desert during the King's Camel Race, in Saudi Arabia. Anyone with a camel to ride may enter. The racers assemble in the city of Riyadh. Then they ride bareback across 14 miles (23 km) of desert sand. In 1980, the year of this competition, 2,704 riders entered. The winning camel galloped over the course in 42 minutes.

ROBERT AZZI/WOODFIN CAMP & ASSOCIATES

Heads Up

You can recognize some kinds of birds by the shapes of their wings and bodies. Other birds have colors or patterns that make them easy to spot. You can't mistake a bluejay or a robin, even if you see it for only an instant.

You don't have to see some birds to identify them. Unusual calls give them away. You can easily recognize an unseen bobwhite or a whippoorwill.

Clues to their identity help birds as well as bird-watchers. Birds must find and recognize others of their kind. Otherwise they would never be able to mate and to raise young.

All the birds on these pages have heads that are special. One look at these far-out heads, and you'd know them anywhere!

"All right, who set the blow dryer on high?" Fluffed-out feathers make the rockhopper penguin look windblown (below). Rockhoppers display their crests of feathers when they are courting mates. They are one of the smaller penguins. Adults stand about 24 inches tall (61 cm). They swim in cool waters north of Antarctica and come ashore on rocky islands to nest. Like other penguins, rockhoppers cannot fly. They move on land by making short hops from rock to rock. People who saw them hopping gave them their name.

"Maybe a little less eyeliner and a little more lipstick?" If puffins have bright bills (right), it must be spring. The colors help the puffins attract mates. Every spring, Atlantic puffins mate and nest along the northern coasts of North America and Europe. At that time, they have colorful plates on their bills. After the puffins have raised their chicks, they go to sea and join large flocks. There, the adults shed their bill plates. During the winter, the puffins spend all their time on or in the water. They feed on small fish. They even sleep at sea, floating on the surface. Adult puffins are 10 to 12 inches tall (25 to 30 cm).

"I just washed it, and I can't do a thing with it." This rooster, called a Polish cock, has a wild crest of feathers. Chicken farmers developed the crest by breeding selected birds. The extra-long feathers are supposed to fall to the sides, as these do. That way, they don't block the rooster's vision or get wet when the bird drinks. The fancy feathers serve only one purpose—to help the birds' owners win prizes in poultry shows.

"My friends say I'm always trying to horn in." The rhinoceros hornbill (below) has a long, hard growth on its bill called a casque (KASK). The casque helps it attract a mate. Adult rhinoceros hornbills stand about 3¹/₂ feet tall (1 m). They live in the southeastern part of Asia.

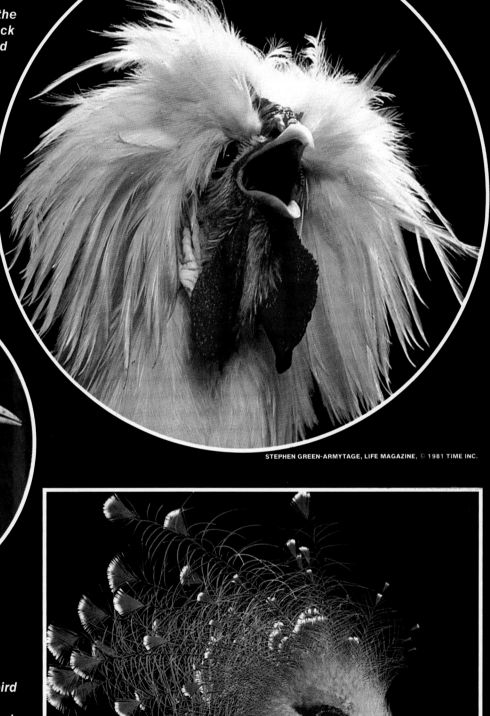

STEPHEN GREEN-ARMYTAGE, LIFE MAGAZINE, © 1981 TIME INC.

WERNER H. MÜLLER FROM PETER ARNOLD, INC.

"... so I said, 'This time I want a style that's really different.' " It's easy to see how the crowned pigeon (right) got its name. This bird doesn't look anything like the pigeons that live in cities. Long feathers on its head fan out, forming a crest. Crowned pigeons are unlike city pigeons in other ways, too. They are about as big as large chickens. They spend most of their time on the ground, gathering food. Crowned pigeons live only in the forests of New Guinea, an island near Australia.

TOM MYERS

Amazing Insects

As a group, insects may be the world's greatest success story. Fossils show that these tiny creatures lived on earth millions of years before larger animals did. Insects survived—and their numbers increased—while some larger animals, such as dinosaurs, died out. Insects live nearly everywhere, under all kinds of conditions. Scientists say that three out of every four creatures now living on earth are insects.

How have insects survived in such great numbers? Disguises help. An inchworm, by instinct, knows how to disguise itself. It chews off bits of flower petals and plasters them over its body. Other insects don't have to work to hide. They're born wearing disguises. Their skins, shells, or scales match the leaves, flowers, twigs, or bark on which they spend their time. This makes it hard for their enemies to find them. You will learn more about the secrets of insect survival on the next pages.

This inchworm may be a doormat, but it won't be a dinner (above). The inchworm is right under the feet of a hungry crab spider. The spider doesn't see it. An inchworm is a small, hairless caterpillar. As it feeds on flowers, it bites off bits of petals. Then it sticks the bits on the back of its body. The disguise conceals it from spiders and from other enemies. The spider's yellow coloring helps it hide from its own enemies. A hungry bird may not spot the spider on the yellow flower. Some people call the inchworm a looper because of the way it moves. As it pulls up its back feet to its front feet, its body rises in a tall loop.

N.G.S. PHOTOGRAPHER ROBERT F. SISSON (ALL)

Yellow and black: stay back! The body of a "wasp" (right) warns enemies to keep away. Birds and other creatures that eat insects fear the bite and sting of the wasp. They usually leave it alone. This insect, however, is not a wasp. It's a different insect called a mantispid (man-TIS-pid). Some kinds of mantispids look like wasps — and act like them as well. Scientists call such creatures mimics, because they mimic, or imitate, others. Wasps have many mimics. One, a kind of hover fly, even makes a buzzing sound similar to the one a wasp makes.

Which of the three butterflies on this wild plant (below) is a mimic? A pipe-vine swallowtail feeds on a flower at the top left. Birds avoid this kind of butterfly because it tastes bad. The butterfly at the top right looks very similar, but it doesn't taste bad. This mimic is a female yellow tiger swallowtail. Its pipe-vine coloring helps protect it from birds. The male yellow tiger swallowtail below them shows the usual coloring of its kind. Not all females have the pipe-vine coloring. Males never do. Scientists aren't certain why some butterflies are mimics and others are not.

The damaged wing of a male yellow tiger swallowtail (below) shows what often happens to good-tasting butterflies that don't mimic bad-tasting ones. Scientists did an experiment with moths to see whether butterfly mimicry worked. They painted the wings of some moths in the usual colors of the good-tasting yellow tiger swallowtail butterflies. They painted the wings of other moths to resemble bad-tasting butterflies. Then they released the moths. Birds attacked the moths that looked like yellow tiger swallowtails more often than they attacked the other moths.

Double-duty wings help the gray comma butterfly survive. When the butterfly rests on a log and folds its wings (right), the undersides of the wings look drab and rough. They match the tree bark perfectly. This makes the gray comma hard to see. When the butterfly seeks a mate, it sits with its wings spread out (below). The bright orange and black colors on the tops of the wings make the butterfly easy for another gray comma to spot. If enemies should spot it as well, the markings may prevent an attack. They resemble the markings of the monarch butterfly. Monarchs taste bad. Birds usually avoid them.

JOHN SHAW (ABOVE RIGHT AND BELOW)

PETER G. AITKEN

A bug-size bedroll keeps this leaf-rolling caterpillar snug and safe from enemies (above). Until it becomes a moth, the caterpillar will live in this rolled-up leaf. To form the shelter, the insect spins silk threads. It attaches the threads to make a mat across a leaf. Air dries the threads. As the threads harden, they shrink. This causes the leaf to roll up with the caterpillar inside.

Chirping at the entrance to its burrow, an East African cricket lifts its wings (right). Crickets make chirping sounds by rubbing together the front parts of their wings. Rough files and scrapers cover the wings where they overlap. The rounded wings of the cricket act somewhat like a cheerleader's megaphone. They make the sounds louder. Some crickets can be heard a mile (1^1/$_2$ km) away. Only male crickets chirp. They usually do it to attract females. A chirp is actually three very high notes. Humans hear the notes as one sound. If another male comes near a chirping cricket, the chirps grow louder and sharper. Sometimes the two males fight. They bite, kick, and lash each other with their feelers. The winner of a cricket fight chirps loudly when the contest ends. Crickets chirp only when darkness hides them from enemies. To make this picture, the photographer used a flashing light.

E. S. ROSS

The bristles on this gypsy moth caterpillar (below) look uninviting—and they are. The bristles contain a chemical called histamine. If you brush against them, the chemical will irritate your skin. You'd think the irritating bristles would discourage animal enemies, too. However some birds, such as the starling and the cuckoo, eat the caterpillars anyway. When the linings of the birds' stomachs become filled with bristles, the birds shed their stomach linings and start over. One enemy, the white-footed mouse (right), avoids the bristles in another way. It peels the caterpillar like a banana and eats only the insides.

DRU COLBERT

DWIGHT KUHN

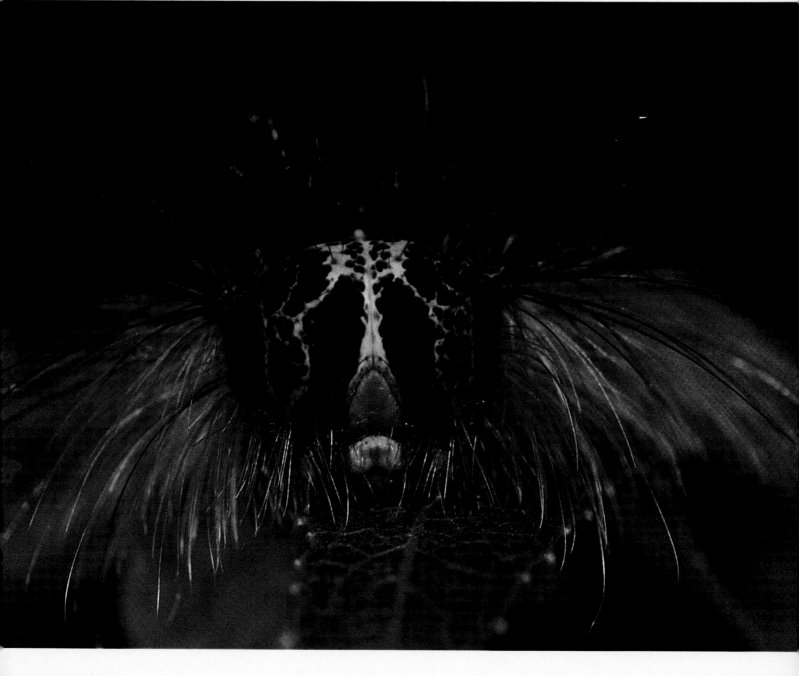

Twinkling insects light up this tree in Malaysia. About once a second, thousands of male fireflies create a flickering display. They give two fast flashes of their tiny lights, all at the same time. Scientists say that this light show may help males attract mates — or it may be just a group activity. Other kinds of fireflies use their lights in different ways. Some don't blink at all but produce a steady glow. In much of the United States, different kinds of fireflies have their own flashing codes. A male rises from the grass just after sunset and flashes the code of his kind. On the ground, a female of the same kind flashes an answering code. You often can get male fireflies to land on your flashlight. Hold the light near the ground and copy a female's answering flash.

A firefly's built-in lantern glows on the underside of its body. Chemicals made by cells in the insect's body produce the glow.

Growing, Growing, Gone

Not all plants begin life as seeds. A few may skip the seed stage. This plant, called a kalanchoe (kal-an-кон-ee), often forms buds along the edges of its leaves. Each bud becomes a tiny plantlet with its own set of leaves and roots.

When the plantlets are ready to grow on their own, they drop from the leaf to the ground. The roots take hold. Soon a family of young plants grows around the parent.

The kalanchoe comes from Africa. People in many places grow it as a houseplant. In its native home, the kalanchoe endures months of rain followed by long dry periods. Some scientists think that producing plantlets helps the kalanchoe survive these harsh conditions. The plantlets drop off during the rainy season. They grow quickly, before the dry spell sets in. By that time, they have well-developed root systems, so they can draw moisture from deep in the earth.

The kalanchoe has many other names. People sometimes call it "air plant," "curtain plant," or "Mexican love plant." The last two names come from a tradition that exists in some Latin American countries. A girl pins a leaf from this plant to her bedroom curtains. She gives each plantlet on the leaf the name of one of her boyfriends. Then she watches as the plantlets drop off. Finally, only one remains. That one tells her the name of the boy she should marry.

C. Allan Morgan

Yellowstone: A Walk-through Volcano

Lakes of colored mud bubble and pop. The ground steams, hisses, and trembles. Geysers send jets of hot water and vapor high into the air. Tiny plants of many colors fill steaming pools. The plants look like rainbows in the water.

Every year, millions of people flock to Yellowstone National Park to see these natural wonders. As they explore, they walk and drive through an ancient volcanic crater. The volcano blew its top thousands of years ago.

In Yellowstone, very high heat from the earth's interior comes closer to a large area of the surface than at any other spot on the continents of the world. Hot water and steam, in the form of springs and geysers, burst out of cracks in the earth.

Underground heat led to the area's name. When visitors look down into the canyon of the Yellowstone River, they see walls of yellow stone. Long ago, hot liquids containing minerals rose through brown or gray stone. The minerals turned the stone yellow. On these pages, you'll explore America's first national park, where earth's inner heat creates special effects.

PAUL CHESLEY

Grand Prismatic Spring, Yellowstone's largest hot spring, shows its colors from above (right). Visitors go right to the water's edge on a boardwalk. You can see the boardwalk near the top of the picture. It gives visitors a close look at the bright colors created by small plants called algae (AL-gee). Yellow algae grow well in hot water. Orange and brown algae grow in slightly cooler temperatures. At the center, the water stays clear and blue. It is too hot there for algae to survive. Magma, melted rock deep inside the earth, heats the underground water that feeds this spring.

Yellowstone has room for small wonders, too. The wolf spider (right) eats tiny flies that live on mats of algae in the park's hot pools and streams. In winter, wolf spiders stay on a narrow strip of ground beside the steaming springs. If the spiders leave this warm area, the freezing temperatures will kill them. Spiders and flies live in the warm areas all year round.

DICK DURRANCE II

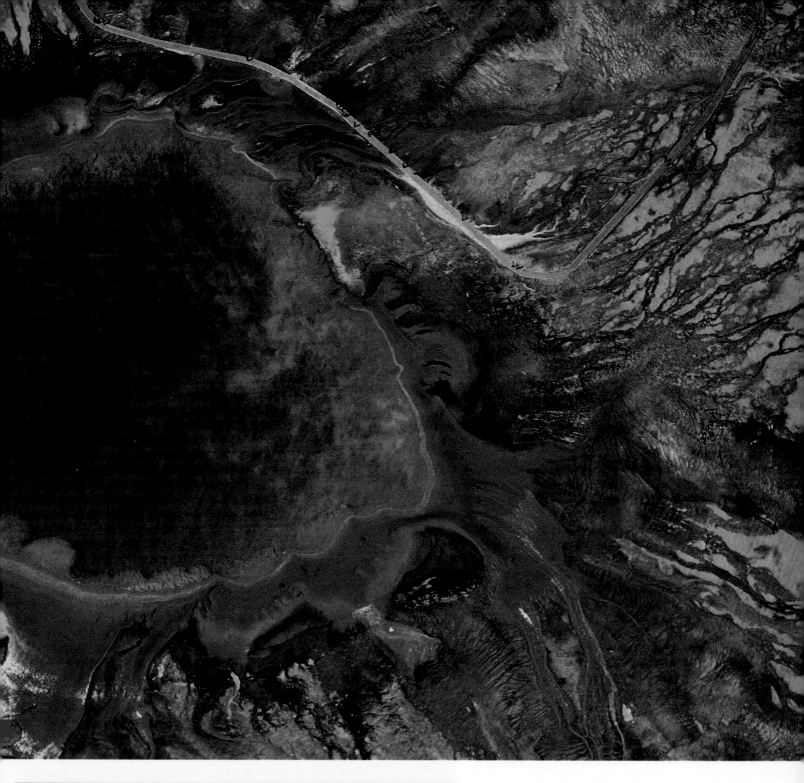

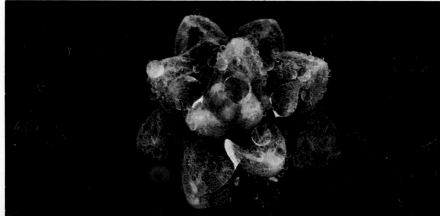

January above, July below. Frost glazes the top half of a pussytoes plant (left). It grows near a hot spring in Yellowstone. Its bottom half is as green as summer grass. Thick moss and a tiny red mushroom also grow in ground warmed by the water. Even though winter has buried the rest of the park in snow, warm areas around hot springs and streams stay full of plant and insect life.

DICK DURRANCE II

Mineral formations that look like giant toadstools grow in the pool around the mouth of Great Fountain Geyser (left). The formation in the front measures about 3 feet across (1 m). Underground water must pass through many layers of rock before it reaches the earth's surface. On the way, the hot water dissolves minerals from the rocks. Water spraying out of the geyser constantly adds minerals to the pool around it. Over thousands of years, these mineral deposits have formed strange shapes. In the past, souvenir hunters cut off pieces of the formations with knives and hatchets. Now laws forbid people to destroy natural materials or to take them from the park.

Emma Fuller, 8, (above) lives in Yellowstone. If you came across an object like the one she is holding, you might think you had discovered an arrowhead. Actually, it's a V-shaped pine needle with a heavy coating of minerals. In Yellowstone, mineral coatings change the shapes of many ordinary things. The minerals come from the water that sprays from geysers. When the water evaporates, mineral deposits remain.

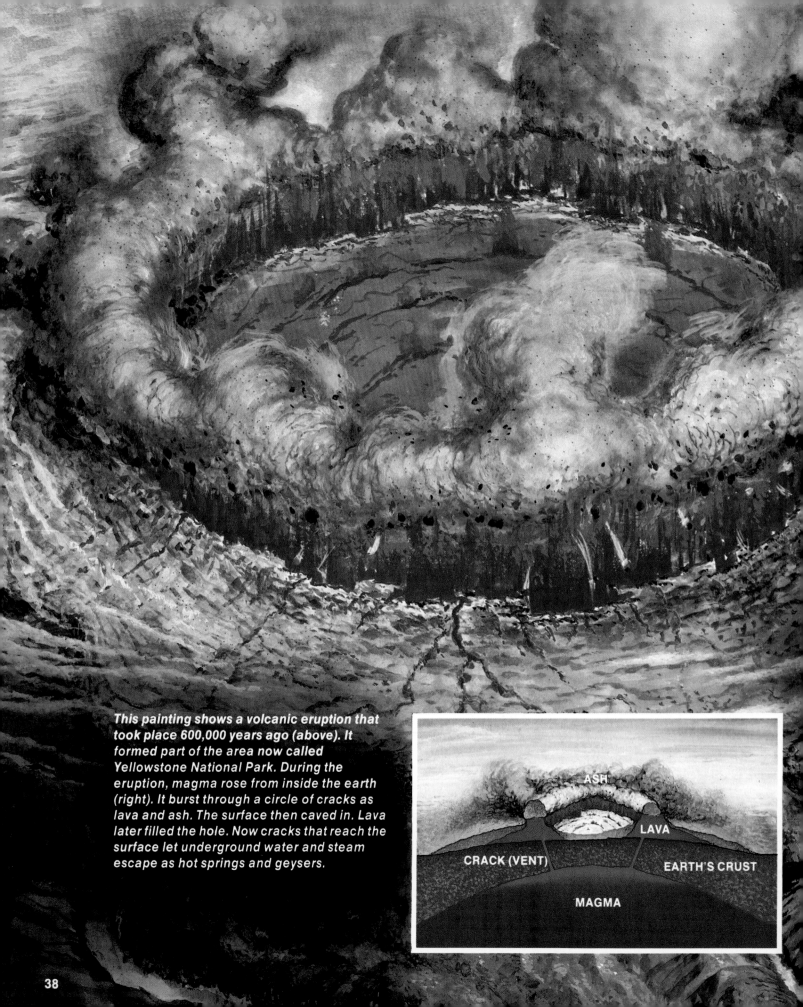

This painting shows a volcanic eruption that took place 600,000 years ago (above). It formed part of the area now called Yellowstone National Park. During the eruption, magma rose from inside the earth (right). It burst through a circle of cracks as lava and ash. The surface then caved in. Lava later filled the hole. Now cracks that reach the surface let underground water and steam escape as hot springs and geysers.

ASH

LAVA

CRACK (VENT)

EARTH'S CRUST

MAGMA

The big boom!

Thousands of centuries ago, a huge explosion shook the area now called Yellowstone National Park. Geologists believe underground pressure caused the volcanic eruption. Geologists are scientists who study the earth and its makeup. This is how they think the explosion occurred:

Magma, or melted rock, built up deep in the earth. It rose to within a few thousand feet of the surface. The pressure of the magma made the surface bulge. A dome formed and began to crack. Some cracks reached down to the magma.

When that happened, huge amounts of magma shot upward through the cracks and exploded into the air. The force of the explosions turned the magma into ash. The ash covered thousands of square miles. In some places, it piled hundreds of feet deep.

The eruption left an empty space under the ground where the magma had been. A roof of rock still covered the space. But soon the roof fell in. It collapsed a mile ($1\frac{1}{2}$ km) downward. The collapse made a crater 40 miles long (64 km) and 30 miles wide (48 km). Geologists call this kind of crater a caldera (kall-DEH-ruh). Lava later filled it.

In Spanish, the word *caldera* means caldron, or cooking pot. A visitor watching the bubbling springs and steaming mud of Yellowstone National Park can easily imagine the place as a huge boiling pot.

Geologists did not discover that Yellowstone National Park contains a caldera until 1956. Lava covered the evidence of the old explosion. Wind and weather wore down most of the caldera rim.

Geologists think two huge volcanic eruptions shook this area before the big boom described here. Will the earth explode at Yellowstone National Park again? Scientists think it might, but they can't predict when it will happen. The earth will give plenty of warning, however. It will shake and swell. Geysers and hot springs will act differently. If another big boom occurs, scientists will not be taken by surprise.

MARVIN J. FRYER

When volcanoes erupt, very high heat and pressure turn rock into flying ash. After the Yellowstone eruption long ago, millions of tons of ash darkened the sky over North America. The map (below) shows where scientists think winds carried the ash. They believe this explosion was a thousand times more powerful than the 1980 eruption of Mount St. Helens, in Washington.

Winter in Yellowstone

Late in October, the first snow begins to fall in Yellowstone National Park. Soon temperatures drop below zero. Strong winds whip heavy snowfalls into huge drifts. Snow blocks the roads. The long Yellowstone winter has begun. It will last until late April.

Winter doesn't stop visitors from coming to the park. On snowshoes and on cross-country skis, they explore a spooky landscape. Spray that falls from geysers freezes within moments. It forms strange-looking ice sculptures. Ice covers nearby trees, bending them into odd shapes.

Clouds of steam hang above ponds that stay warm all winter. Bright algae in hot springs provide spots of color in white fields of snow. In places where warm water runs off from these ponds and springs, small plants grow all winter long. Insects buzz and hop around the plants as if it were summer.

These curious things happen at Yellowstone because of the magma under the earth and the cracks in its surface. Wherever hot water and steam rise to the surface, the nearby ground stays warm. In spite of sub-zero temperatures, mosses and grasses grow on these warm patches of ground. Bison, elk, moose, and deer use such spots as their winter feeding grounds.

STEVEN FULLER (BOTH)

Ice crystals glitter in the sun near a steaming geyser pool (above). In winter, windblown spray freezes into fantastic shapes when it meets the cold ground. Rangers warn visitors to stay out of the path of windblown spray. The water cools quickly as it falls. It will give the visitors a cold shower instead of the warm shower they may expect. The water from geysers will also ruin their camera lenses and eyeglasses. It contains silica, a mineral that sticks to glass.

Like big blobs of whipped cream, snow-covered rocks lie on the bare ground near a geyser (left). When snow falls on the warm earth around a geyser or hot spring, it melts as soon as it hits the ground. But when snow falls on large, cold objects such as rocks, it sticks. People call the white blobs "snow eggs" or "snow mushrooms."

Steam and hot water spray from Castle Geyser. Geysers erupt when an underground steam explosion forces hot water through a narrow opening to the surface. The eruption releases the pressure. Then the geyser quiets down for a while. Castle Geyser shoots water 90 feet (27 m) into the air for nearly 20 minutes. Then it spouts steam for an hour. It takes about 10 hours for underground pressure to build back up to the point where it causes another explosion. Yellowstone Park has 70 large geysers. They spout water 10 feet (3 m) or more. The park also holds 130 smaller geysers. Old Faithful is the most famous. It "faithfully" erupts on a fairly regular schedule, every 50 to 90 minutes.

EARTH SCENES/MARK NEWMAN

Happy Birthday

Walk through an American town on any afternoon, and you're likely to pass a house with a bunch of balloons tied to the doorknob. That's a sure sign that a birthday party is going on inside, complete with cake, candles, ice cream, games, and—of course—presents.

If you were in another country, however, a birthday party might have none of these things. People celebrate birthdays in many different ways. In China, children have parties every year, but adults celebrate only once every ten years. Some people in Africa and Asia don't celebrate birthdays at all.

The custom of having a yearly party with cake, presents, and all the trimmings began in Germany hundreds of years ago. The *Kinderfest,* or children's party, soon spread to other parts of Europe. Later, it spread to places where Europeans traveled and settled, such as the American colonies.

Americans added the familiar birthday song. In 1893, two Kentucky sisters—both teachers—composed "Happy Birthday to You" for their students. Now people sing it in many parts of the world.

1. Video fever! Partygoers in the United States often replace traditional games with more modern ones. They hold their celebrations at electronic-game arcades. Even space-age parties usually include cake, candles, and the singing of "Happy Birthday to You."

2. Gifts for guests. At the end of a birthday party in England, guests dig into a tub of sawdust for favors. Some find valuable prizes. Others get things that are useless or just plain silly. Each guest takes a turn at the "lucky dip" tub—and each hopes for the best.

SUE LEVIN

3. Piñata (peen-YAHT-uh) party. In Mexico, a blindfolded birthday boy or girl uses a stick to break open a papier-mâché animal filled with candy and favors. An adult raises and lowers the piñata to make the game harder.

4. *Bedside birthday.* A Swedish child's celebration begins early. The whole family troops in with gifts the first thing in the morning.

5. *Paper decorations.* In the Netherlands, family and friends honor a child's birthday by making fancy paper cutouts called *slingers*. These colorful cutouts decorate the child's home and classroom on the big day.

6. *Make a wish!* Blowing out candles on a cake first became popular in Germany. People believed the candles had the magic power to make wishes come true.

7. *Spill the candy.* At birthday parties in Italy, children play a game much like the Mexican piñata game. Blindfolded, they try to hit a candy-filled basket, called a *pignatta* (peen-YAHT-uh).

8. *"I hope I live to be a hundred!"* In China, long noodles stand for long life. On their birthdays, people eat and give away bowls of long noodles.

9. *What will the baby grow up to be?* In Korea, the first birthday party may give a clue. The baby sits at a table covered with objects. The object the baby picks up first foretells the future.

10. *Kite ceremony.* At 13, a Japanese boy gets a kite with his name on it. Relatives and friends knot strings together to fly the kite. The boy gives each knot a look of silent thanks for what that person has done for him. Then he lets the kite go.

11. *Happy birthday to us.* In the tiny kingdom of Bhutan, northeast of India, everyone officially becomes a year older on new year's day.

12. *Happy birthday to others.* In Thailand, children give presents on their birthdays instead of receiving them. A Thai child might give food to a monk or buy a caged bird and set it free.

Fun-tastic Foods

This American flag will never fly from any flagpole. It's a cake large enough to feed at least 76,000 people! Hundreds of chefs worked on the cake. It set a world record for size in 1980.

Although a giant cake like this one might be your idea of the perfect food, it wouldn't suit everyone. What people eat is a matter of taste. If you had been born in France, you might be fond of eating frog legs, or snails cooked in butter and garlic. For people in Japan, slices of raw fish fresh from the sea are a treat. So are candied grasshoppers. In China, people sometimes eat cooked bear paws. If you went to another country, the local food might seem strange. But in many places, people would be puzzled if you offered them a pizza, pretzels, or a peanut-butter sandwich. Turn the page to see what's cooking around the world.

A team of chefs cooks up some patriotism with a star-spangled cake (below). The chefs served the 19,000-pound (8,618-kg) cake to people in Peekskill, New York, to raise money for a local health center. Bakers in a nearby town mixed and baked the yellow batter. They took it to Peekskill in a large truck. A second bakery provided batches of red, white, and blue frosting. In Peekskill, chefs spread the

frosting on 2,000 separate squares of cake (above, left). Then they arranged the squares on a wooden platform (above, right). Putting it all together was no piece of cake. A hundred chefs worked five hours just to frost and assemble the cake. The tricky part was making sure it turned out looking like a flag. An engineer drew up plans for the chefs to follow. In the end, the flag was perfect. The

chefs who helped with the cake are old hands at creating giant food displays. One year, they cracked 10,000 eggs to cook the world's largest omelette. Another time, they packed meats, cheeses, and other fillings into a sandwich more than a thousand feet long (305 m). In 1981, they prepared the world's largest popcorn ball. Twelve feet across (4 m), it was made of caramel corn.

JAMES CYPHER/GLOBE PHOTOS

Two Japanese girls share a holiday lunch (left). The girls took a trip by train to see blossoming cherry trees. At a train station along the way, they bought box lunches called eki-ben (ee-kee-BEN). The girl on the left uses chopsticks to hold a serving of sushi (SUE-she). The sushi consists of strips of raw fish inside a ball of rice. Horseradish makes the sushi spicy. A strip of dried black seaweed holds it together. Wherever the train makes a stop, passengers can buy eki-ben containing the local food specialties. Some Japanese enjoy eki-ben so much that they take train trips just to sample box lunches from different parts of the country.

PAUL CHESLEY

Oh, my, what a pie! Kathy Sawicki, of Washington, D. C., cuts the first slice from a huge strawberry pie (below). People in a busy park ate 5,000 pieces of this giant dessert in 1979. In return for pieces of pie, the people gave money to a hospital for children. More than a ton (1 t) of strawberries went into the pie. When the pie was put together, it measured 20 by 40 feet (6 by 12 m). Bakers used a hundred cans of whipped cream to decorate individual servings as they were handed out. In less than an hour after the first slice was cut, the entire pie was gone.

N.G.S. PHOTOGRAPHER JOSEPH H. BAILEY

Sweet treat. A Mexican boy chews sugarcane fresh from his father's farm (left). Using a large knife, the boy's father chopped down a cane stalk and cut off a small section. The father trimmed away the cane's tough skin. Beneath the skin lies the juicy pulp. The boy bites off a mouthful of pulp. Then he chews it for its sweet taste. When the juice and taste are gone, he spits out the pulp and takes another bite. Sugarcane is a kind of grass that grows as tall as 20 feet (6 m) in hot, wet climates. The sugar you use at home probably came from sugarcane.

Looking like empty balloons, octopuses dry in the sun in Greece (above). To catch them, swimmers wade or dive in the sea and pull the creatures from their hiding places. People tenderize the tough octopus meat by beating it on rocks. Then they hang the meat up to dry. Weeks later, they soak bite-size chunks of octopus meat in water and broil the chunks as tasty snacks.

Tired of tomatoes? How about a colorful salad of orange marigolds, red and white hollyhocks, purple violets, and other flowers (left). Lamb's-quarters, a plant with tall clusters of tiny seeds and spinach-like leaves, adds crunch. Eating flowers is not a new idea. American Indians thickened their soups and stews by dropping squash blossoms into the pot. Of course, not all flowers are good—or safe—to eat. If you want to make a flower salad, ask an adult who knows how to choose the ingredients to help you.

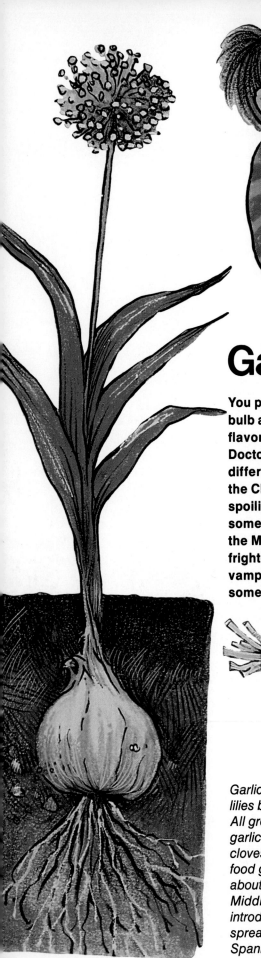

Rub a piece of garlic on the sole of your foot (left). In just a few minutes, other people will smell garlic on your breath. Garlic oil passes through your skin into your blood. The blood carries it to your lungs, and some of the odor escapes as you breathe.

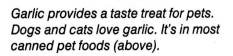

Garlic: Spice of Life

You probably have seen garlic in the kitchen. It's a bulb about the size of a small onion, and it's filled with flavor. But people prize garlic for more than its taste. Doctors in ancient Rome recommended garlic for 61 different problems, including snakebite. In the 1200s, the Chinese rubbed garlic on meat to keep it from spoiling. People used garlic for so many things that some thought the plant had magical powers. During the Middle Ages, some Europeans believed it frightened away vampires. Of course, there are no vampires, so this couldn't be true. Here you'll read some garlic facts even stranger than garlic fiction.

Garlic provides a taste treat for pets. Dogs and cats love garlic. It's in most canned pet foods (above).

Want to open up a stuffy nose? Some people suggest boiling garlic in water and inhaling the steam (below). For centuries, people have used garlic to help relieve the symptoms of the common cold. Many people in the Soviet Union chew garlic as a cure for the flu. In fact, some people call this plant "Russian penicillin." Garlic does kill germs, including some kinds of germs that resist antibiotics. During World War I, doctors put garlic on wounds to help stop infection.

Garlic (above and left), onions, and lilies belong to the same plant family. All grow from bulbs. You can divide a garlic bulb into small pieces called cloves. The kind of garlic that seasons food grew first in Central Asia. By about 5,000 years ago, people in the Middle East were using it. They introduced it to Italy. Roman soldiers spread it throughout Europe. Later, Spanish explorers took it to America.

WILLIAM COULTER

This Roman soldier (below) has a smelly secret weapon. Before going into battle, he eats garlic. Romans believed that garlic gave them strength and courage, which would help them overcome their enemies. Garlic won't really make you brave, but it does contain vitamins and minerals. It also helps the body absorb other vitamins.

Garlic soup and a crackling fire keep Father Jacques Marquette warm during a cold winter (above). In 1674, bad health forced Father Marquette, a French missionary and explorer, to spend the winter near a place called "Checagou." That's an Indian word meaning "place of garlic." Eating the wild garlic saved him from scurvy. Now people call the place Chicago.

● An ancient writer said that builders of the Great Pyramid in Egypt went on strike when their garlic supply was reduced. A good part of the workers' diet consisted of garlic, onions, radishes, and bread.

● Siberian citizens considered garlic so valuable during the 17th and 18th centuries that they paid their taxes with it.

● Eleanor Roosevelt, wife of President Franklin D. Roosevelt, ate three chocolate-covered garlic balls every morning. Her doctor had suggested the garlic to improve her memory.

● A spray of garlic, oil, soap, and water kills pests such as mosquitoes and flies.

Yo, ho, ho, and a clove of garlic! Vikings took garlic on sea voyages (right). It stays fresh for a long time, and it is rich in vitamin C. This vitamin prevents a disease called scurvy.

Machines That 'Think'

You drop in a quarter, and PAC-MAN races across the screen, gobbling dots as he goes. Blinky appears, and the chase is on. You jiggle the control stick, trying to outsmart him. Bip, bip, bip, bip, bip, bip—gulp! Your hero wilts, whines, and disappears. You've lost this round to a smart, speedy machine—the computer.

Computers process information so fast that people don't measure their speed in seconds. They measure it in billionths of a second, or nanoseconds. No wonder people keep finding more and more jobs for computers to do!

You probably take these electronic thinking machines for granted. Yet computers may be no older than your parents. The first machine with an electronic memory was invented in 1946. It was huge—the size of a gym. It was expensive to build and complicated to operate. Specially trained people had to translate questions into code and feed the code into the computer. When the computer printed out answers, they were also in code. Specialists had to translate them into everyday language.

All that has changed. Engineers have made computers smaller, cheaper, and more efficient. Some computers now have partners—picture screens and simple controls. A programmed computer and its partners form a computer-graphics system. With a little instruction, anyone can use such a system.

A video game is one example of a computer-graphics system at work. A programmed computer changes information into pictures. An operator communicates with the computer by drawing, by typing, by pressing switches and buttons, or by using other hand controls. The computer responds by turning the message into a picture. When the picture flashes on the screen, the operator can tell the machine to make changes.

Using a computer-graphics system, an architect can design a skyscraper quickly and accurately. At the same time, the computer can record a list of materials needed to construct the building. Using that list and other information, the computer can estimate the cost of the building. It can even be programmed to show people the views they will have from their windows.

Artists use computer-graphics systems in a variety of ways. They can instruct a system to make step-by-step drawings for animated movies—in a fraction of the time it takes humans to make such drawings. Computer-graphics systems draw complicated maps, combining information from many sources. They change lists of numbers into graphs and charts.

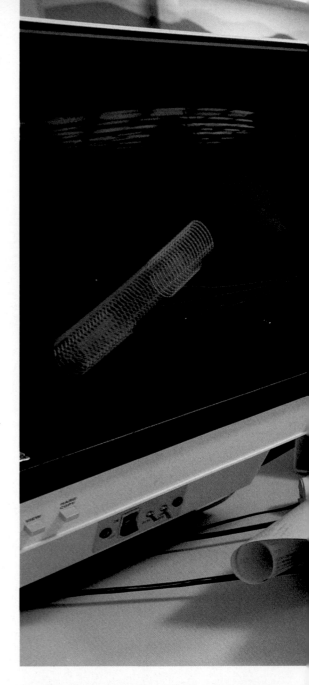

Norman Apperson (above) tells a computer how to draw the fuselage, or body, of a Boeing 767 airplane. In his right hand, Apperson holds a tool called a digitizing puck. He moves the puck along the lines of a drawing of a fuselage. He stops his hand often and presses a button. The puck transmits its location on the drawing to the computer. The computer draws lines connecting the location points, and a picture of the fuselage takes shape on the screen. The Boeing 767 has more than a hundred thousand parts. Before engineers had computer-graphics systems, they drew the same part many times to show it from different angles. Now they do one drawing. They feed it into the computer, with instructions. The computer does the rest of the drawings for them.

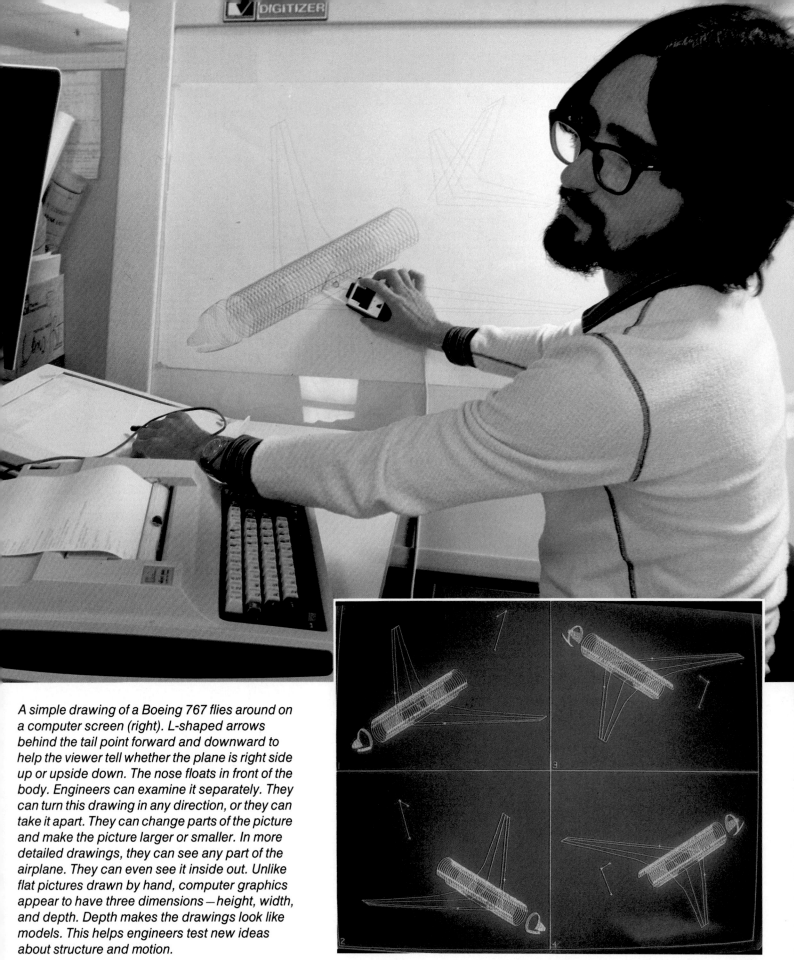

A simple drawing of a Boeing 767 flies around on a computer screen (right). L-shaped arrows behind the tail point forward and downward to help the viewer tell whether the plane is right side up or upside down. The nose floats in front of the body. Engineers can examine it separately. They can turn this drawing in any direction, or they can take it apart. They can change parts of the picture and make the picture larger or smaller. In more detailed drawings, they can see any part of the airplane. They can even see it inside out. Unlike flat pictures drawn by hand, computer graphics appear to have three dimensions — height, width, and depth. Depth makes the drawings look like models. This helps engineers test new ideas about structure and motion.

JAMES A. SUGAR (BOTH)

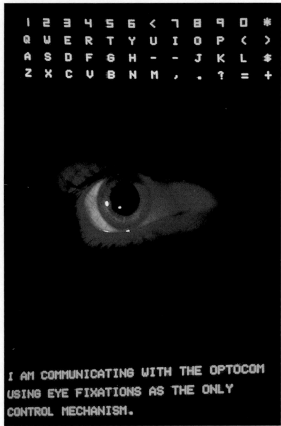

I AM COMMUNICATING WITH THE OPTOCOM USING EYE FIXATIONS AS THE ONLY CONTROL MECHANISM.

DAN MCCOY FROM RAINBOW (ABOVE AND BELOW, RIGHT)

See and say. That's what this computer does (above). A person can command it just by looking at it. To operate the computer, you simply look at each letter and symbol that you want to print. The computer records your eye movements. When your eye pauses, the computer prints that letter or symbol. The system is called OptoCom. Two scientists designed it for handicapped people who cannot use a regular typewriter keyboard. After practicing with the system, volunteers could use it to type 13 words a minute.

When an operator talks to this computer (right), it talks back. Engineers are beginning to program computers to understand human speech. It's a tough job. No two voices are alike. People who speak the same language may say words in different ways. It's hard for computers to tell where words begin and end. Background noise may confuse the machines. Today's computers cannot understand ordinary conversation. People have to be trained to speak to the computers in a certain way. But some machines now can recognize as many as 900 words. Other computers respond to spoken words with spoken words of their own. If you ask for large amounts of information, they type it out.

INFORMATION INTERNATIONAL, INC.

Connect the dots. Have you ever drawn a dot-to-dot picture? A computer used this method to make the picture called "Gallery" (left). First, an artist recorded shapes and objects as position points on a computer screen. Then the artist instructed the computer to draw lines connecting the points. The artist looked at the picture on a screen and made changes in it. It took hundreds of hours to program the computer. The computer produced the finished picture in 15 minutes.

THE NATIONAL CENTER FOR ATMOSPHERIC RESEARCH IS SPONSORED BY THE NATIONAL SCIENCE FOUNDATION

Other kinds of computers do other far-out jobs. They listen to people talk, understand what they say, and type out messages. They read books aloud to blind people. They command vehicles in space. They run machines that produce manufactured parts. They operate certain kinds of processing plants. They check on computer-operated equipment and signal when it needs maintenance work—before the equipment breaks down. Some computers even design other computers.

The machines that do all these things are small compared with their bulky ancestors. An average home computer with a video screen will fit into two large typewriter cases. Many computers are even smaller. Tiny memory chips keep them working. A chip that holds a million bits of information can go through the eye of a large needle.

Present-day computers give the answers to complicated questions in a few seconds. Most people communicate with them by typing. Soon, you won't even have to do that. You'll speak to a computer and get a sensible answer—in a calm electronic voice.

What will the climate on earth be like in 20 years? In 50 years? In 100 years? Computer maps (above) may help scientists make predictions. A computer can combine many maps into one. It can take a map showing physical features of the earth and add photographs from satellites. It can show wind patterns, cloud formations, storm systems, and other changes in the atmosphere — all on one model. Scientists use such models as research tools. They look at the patterns and change some elements on the computer. The computer shows them how each change affects other elements. This helps them forecast what might happen to the earth if certain changes in the atmosphere should actually take place.

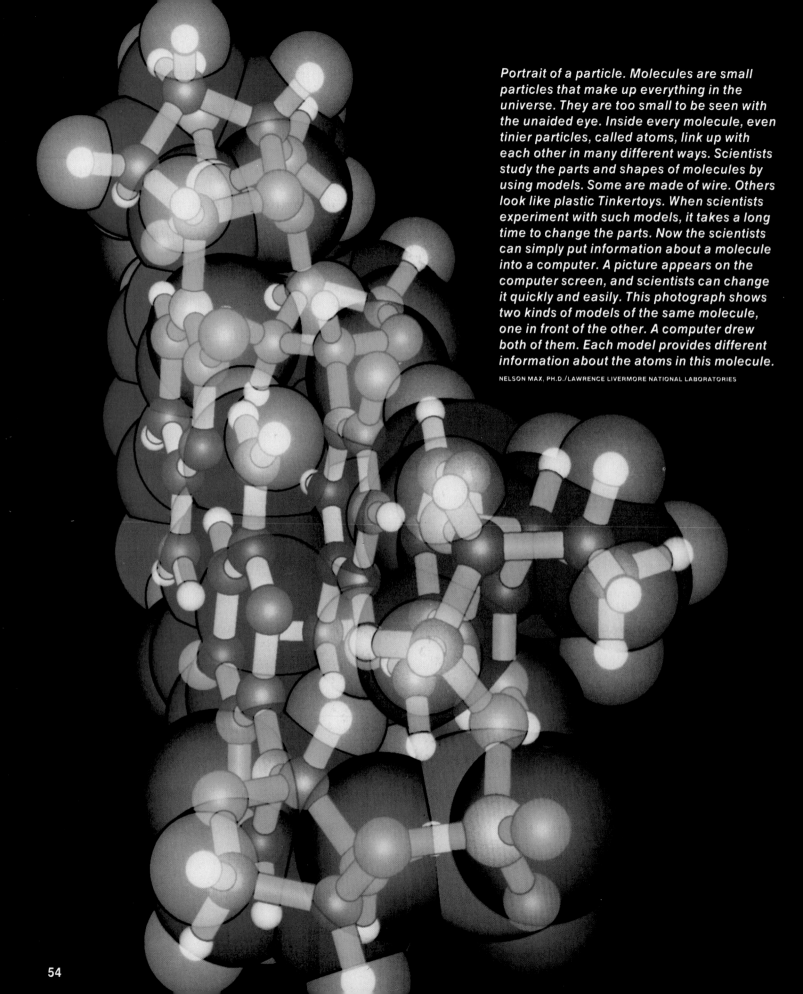

Portrait of a particle. Molecules are small particles that make up everything in the universe. They are too small to be seen with the unaided eye. Inside every molecule, even tinier particles, called atoms, link up with each other in many different ways. Scientists study the parts and shapes of molecules by using models. Some are made of wire. Others look like plastic Tinkertoys. When scientists experiment with such models, it takes a long time to change the parts. Now the scientists can simply put information about a molecule into a computer. A picture appears on the computer screen, and scientists can change it quickly and easily. This photograph shows two kinds of models of the same molecule, one in front of the other. A computer drew both of them. Each model provides different information about the atoms in this molecule.

NELSON MAX, PH.D./LAWRENCE LIVERMORE NATIONAL LABORATORIES

The King's Giraffe

In the palace gardens, a little princess hangs a garland of flowers around the neck of the first giraffe to visit France.

BARBARA GIBSON

It was like a fairy tale come true: an animal from a faraway land calling on a king. It happened in France, in a time still known as the Year of the Giraffe.

In 1826, a wealthy African official sent a female giraffe by ship as a gift to the King of France. Two dairy cows went along to supply the giraffe with fresh milk. The ship docked in southern France. The first giraffe to step on French soil spent the winter as an honored guest of the mayor of Marseilles. When spring came, the long journey continued.

Each day, officials led the giraffe along the road to Paris, the capital of France. Soldiers on horseback held back the crowds. The giraffe, with the cows, slowly walked north. She traveled 500 miles in all (805 km), nibbling leaves from treetops as she went.

On the last day of June in 1827 she arrived in the great city of Paris. In the palace gardens, the royal family officially welcomed the giraffe to Paris. The King, as delighted as anyone at seeing his first giraffe, fed his tall guest a handful of rose petals.

The city went slightly giraffe-crazy. Parisians erected a bronze statue of the animal. They put portraits of giraffes on dinner plates, wallpaper, and candy boxes. They wrote songs about their visitor. People crowded into the Paris Zoo. There the giraffe— gazing down at her admirers— lived happily ever after.

Fish Tricks

When a big fish meets a smaller fish, what usually happens? Gulp! The big fish eats the smaller fish. If you think this makes the underwater world seem like a dangerous place, you're right.

Fish and other sea creatures constantly have to fight for their lives, just as wild animals on land do. Fish use a wide variety of tricks to escape enemies and to catch food.

Many have ways of fooling their enemies. Fish that live among bright corals may have bright coloring. They may be shaped like plants that grow near the reefs. Fish that stay near the seafloor may have dull coloring and flat shapes. A few kinds of fish actually change color when their surroundings change. They can do this because they have special color cells in their skin. Such fish can match their backgrounds almost perfectly.

Some fish swallow water and puff up when attacked. This action makes them look large and fierce. Some produce bad-tasting or

The flashlight fish (above) has lights that blink on and off. A light organ beneath each eye produces the glow. Each light organ contains billions of glowing bacteria. The bacteria shine for hours at a time—even after the fish dies. The flashlight fish uses these built-in lights to help it spot the tiny creatures it eats. It also uses the lights to signal other flashlight fish. If an enemy approaches, the flashlight fish can draw black flaps of skin over its lights. The attacker may think the fish has disappeared. You can find flashlight fish in warm waters in most parts of the world.

DAVID DOUBILET (BOTH)

Dazed by the light from an underwater lamp, a flashlight fish lies quietly in the hand of a diver (right). The diver will take the fish to an aquarium laboratory for study. Flashlight fish are shy and quick to panic. They avoid all light but their own. To catch this one, the diver approached in total darkness. Then he flicked on the lamp and caught the fish.

poisonous substances that cause most other fish to avoid them.

A few fish have built-in lighting systems. The whole body, or a part of it, lights up. Such a fish may produce a steady glow or blink on and off. Scientists think these underwater lights serve several purposes. The lights may help a fish attract food or signal others of its kind. The lights may also confuse enemies.

Certain tricks benefit the young. One fish builds a nest of bubbles for the eggs and guards them. Other fish keep their eggs and babies safe inside pouches or in a large mouth. A few carry the eggs around on their tails. One fish carries strings of eggs attached to a hook on its forehead.

One of these weedy sea dragons is baby-sitting (above). It's the one in the center, with the large cluster of eggs on its tail. This sea dragon is a male. The female lays eggs on the tail of her mate. Then she swims away. The father carries the eggs until they hatch, in about a month. As soon as the young hatch, they can take care of themselves. The weedy sea dragon is a kind of sea horse. Sea dragons live along the coast of Australia. About 18 inches long (46 cm), they look a little like storybook dragons. They also resemble strands of drifting seaweed.

PAUL A. ZAHL, PH.D.

Wrapped in a "nightgown," a parrotfish sleeps (above). At night, an organ behind the fish's head produces a colorless substance somewhat like gelatin. It forms an envelope around the parrotfish that may discourage eels and other larger fish from eating it. Parrotfish live in warm waters in many parts of the world. They get their name from the parrotlike beaks they use to scrape tiny plants off coral reefs. Like all fish, they have no eyelids. They sleep with their eyes open.

Ready, aim . . . spit! And the archerfish does just that (right). Here, it tries to shoot down a beetle. When the fish spots an insect it wants to eat, it stops breathing for a moment and takes in a mouthful of water. It presses its tongue against a groove in its mouth, forming a tube. Then it aims and fires. The jet of water will knock the beetle off the leaf and into the water—near the waiting archerfish. Archerfish live in rivers, streams, and coastal waters in parts of Asia and Australia. They can spit jets of water 10 feet (3 m) into the air. They can even shoot down insects in flight.

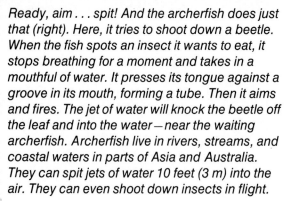

New Parts for Old

A lizard darts through the underbrush looking for insects to eat. As it hunts, a bird attacks, grabbing the lizard by its long tail. Things look bad for the lizard. Suddenly its tail comes off in the attacker's mouth. The tailless lizard scurries away to safety.

Many lizards have the ability to part with their tails as a means of self-defense. Over a period of time, they grow new tails. Their new tails are very much like the old ones. This process of regrowth is called regeneration.

Several kinds of animals can grow a new limb if one is lost in an escape, an accident, or a fight. Some worms grow new sections. Starfish grow new arms. Some snails grow new eyes. In Florida, crabbers take advantage of the crab's ability to regenerate. The stone crab, which has tasty claws, became scarce in Florida. Now, by law, people take only the claws of a crab. They throw the crab back into the water. It will grow new claws. Someone else may harvest them later on.

All living things have some ability to replace, or at least to repair, damaged parts. In human beings, the healing of wounds is a kind of regeneration. The human liver can grow back to normal size after being damaged.

Scientists have spent years studying regeneration. They hope someday to understand enough about the process to find more ways of helping human beings recover from serious injuries.

Spare Parts Unlimited

▼ *Starfish can regenerate entire parts of their bodies. Some kinds, such as the starfish called* Linckia, *can cast off one or more of their*

ED ROBINSON/TOM STACK & ASSOCIATES

Missing the Point...

One, two, three, grow! In this series of five photographs (right), a small lizard called a gecko grows a new tail. In the first picture, the lizard looks as if it has had a terrible accident. It has lost its tail. Pictures two, three, and four show the tail regenerating. In the fifth picture, it looks as good as new. The lizard probably lost its tail while fleeing from an enemy, such as a bird. Like many lizards, geckos can shed their tails when attacked. After the tail drops off, it lies wriggling on the ground. This motion may confuse the attacker and give the gecko time to escape. When the tail falls off, it breaks away at a section of the body where the bone breaks cleanly. A muscle quickly contracts to stop any bleeding. New cells soon begin to grow near the break. The new growth, called a bud, develops into an entirely new tail. In about eight months to a year, the lizard has a new, full-size tail.

Right after losing its tail

After two to three weeks

arms. Then each arm can grow into a new starfish. While the body is growing at the end of the arm, the animal looks a little like a comet that streaks across the sky. Scientists call this stage of regeneration the comet form. The *Linckia* lives in tropical areas of the Pacific Ocean.

Losing one of its five arms created no problem for this starfish. It simply started to grow a replacement. The ability of starfish to regenerate has caused problems for some people, however. Starfish eat many of the oysters that New England oystermen depend on for their living. Almost a hundred years ago, the oystermen tried to reduce the number of starfish in their area. They collected great numbers of starfish and cut them into pieces. Then, thinking the starfish were dead, they threw them back into the water. Soon the starfish problem was much worse. Starfish that had been cut in half grew into two new animals. Those cut into thirds became three new starfish. Single arms grew new bodies. When the oystermen realized that each piece was growing into a new animal, they stopped cutting up the starfish and left them on shore to die.

After six to eight weeks

After three to four months

After eight to twelve months

Odd Jobs

What do you want to be when you grow up? A doctor, nurse, lawyer, police officer, teacher, fire fighter, secretary, banker, ballet dancer, football player?

How would you like to be an aquarist, a paleontologist, a model maker, an eagle bander, a clown, or a juggler? If you've never thought about these jobs, that's not surprising. They aren't your average, everyday occupations.

All of the people on these pages have unusual jobs. The aquarist (uh-KWAR-ist) helps care for sea creatures. The paleontologist (pay-lee-ahn-TAHL-uh-just) digs up bones and studies them to learn what life on earth was like long ago. The

Swimming with sharks is all part of the day's work for an aquarist. Barbara Bartelt (below) catches a ride on a nurse shark during the weekly tank cleaning at Sea World in Orlando, Florida. Nurse sharks do not attack humans. A net keeps the dangerous sharks in a separate area on cleaning day. Aquarists at Sea World take care of the fish and other sea creatures. They feed them, look after their health, check on the quality of their water, and clean their tanks. Most aquarists have studied marine biology. Many had aquariums of their own when they were children.

MITCH KEZAR

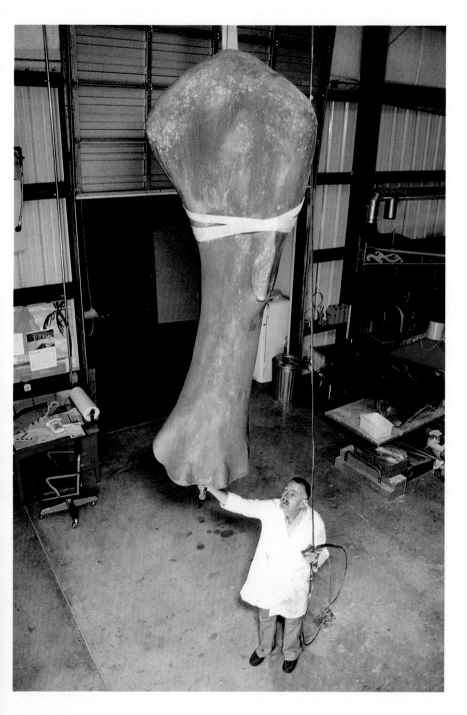

People call him Dinosaur Jim, and with good reason. Dr. James A. Jensen, of Provo, Utah (left), found the bones of the largest dinosaur yet discovered. He calls the dinosaur "Ultrasaurus." Dr. Jensen first spotted bone bits sticking out of a mountainside near Delta, Colorado. He brought in digging equipment and uncovered a shoulder blade 9 feet long (3 m). Later he found other huge remains, such as this 9-foot-long leg bone. Dr. Jensen plans to construct a partial skeleton of Ultrasaurus. He will fill in some of the missing parts with artificial bones. When he has finished, he expects the skeleton to reach to the ceiling of his laboratory. That is 35 feet high (11 m). "I don't have the top end of the neck," he says. "If I had the complete skeleton, it would stand as tall as a six-story building."

WM. FLOYD HOLDMAN

"I used to carve little wooden airplanes with a pocketknife," says Glenn Richer (below), a model maker for Boeing Aircraft, in Seattle, Washington. In a plant filled with space-age technology, Richer does careful hand carving amid shavings and sawdust. From Richer's wooden models, workers make molds for plastic airplanes. Salespeople use the plastic planes in displays.

JAMES A. SUGAR

model maker carves exact copies of the latest airplanes. The eagle bander makes dangerous climbs to help scientists track an endangered species. The clown and the jugglers entertain.

Odd jobs often relate to interests people had as children. The paleontologist dreamed of finding dinosaur bones. The model maker had a knack for whittling wood. The eagle bander spent a lot of time watching birds on his family's farm. The clown made her family and friends laugh.

What do you like to do best? If it's something unusual, perhaps one day you'll have an odd job, too.

The band on the leg of this bald eagle (below) has an identifying number and the address of the U. S. Fish and Wildlife Service. If someone spots this band and reports the number, scientists will find out where the bird went after leaving its nest. Most states classify bald eagles as an endangered species. By learning more about their habits, scientists hope to help the eagles survive. John Holt (right) spends several months a year traveling to nest sites. In the past 14 years, he has banded more than a thousand eagles.

HEINZ KLUETMEIER/SPORTS ILLUSTRATED (BOTH)

In a nest 100 feet (30 m) above the ground, two young bald eagles stare at Holt (right). He climbed this tree using only a rope, and iron spurs on his shoes. Holt has a permit to handle endangered birds. He scrambles up a tall tree by looping a rope around the trunk. He climbs a few feet and throws the rope higher. Then he climbs a few more feet. Once Holt reaches a nest, he ties himself to the tree. Slowly, he reaches toward the birds with his hooked "eagle stick." The bald eagles in this picture are only eight weeks old. They cannot fly yet. If they become frightened, they may leap from the nest and fall to their death. Holt must work carefully. He will grasp each bird with his stick. Then he will gently pull it toward him and attach a band to one leg.

Clowning around, Judy Wall entertains children at a school party in Bethesda, Maryland (right). Her act combines the skills of a clown, a magician, and a sculptor. In a wig and a bright silk costume, she leads parades, does magic tricks, and makes animals from skinny balloons. Then she shows her audience how to make balloon animals of their own. "The fun comes in putting imagination to work," she says. "You can make any kind of animal with balloons." As she blows up each balloon, she stretches it full length. "Ideally, you should inflate the balloon in one big breath, but that's nearly impossible," she says. "I make a tiny bubble to get it started. You have to know when to use lung power and when to use your cheeks." With a twist here and a tie there, Judy can shape a giraffe, a swan, an octopus—or almost any kind of animal you can name. She holds a bumblebee in her right hand and a rabbit in her left (below). Judy now lives and clowns in St. Petersburg, Florida.

The Flying Karamazov Brothers easily keep 12 tenpins in the air. Special lighting captures the action and seems to multiply the tenpins. The Karamazovs juggle many strange things. In one act, they toss around a flaming torch, a cleaver, a champagne bottle, a ukelele, a rubber fish, a corncob pipe, a frying pan, a sickle, and an egg. While juggling, they crack

N.G.S. PHOTOGRAPHER JOSEPH H. BAILEY

the egg into the pan, cook it with the torch, and open the bottle. In another routine, a member of the group tries to juggle any three things members of the audience throw onstage. If he fails, he gets a pie in the face. The jugglers took their name from the title of a Russian book, The Brothers Karamazov, because they liked the sound of it.

Where Dinosaurs Lived and Died

"It was this big." Darren Tanke (below), a scientist, describes a giant prehistoric turtle to young visitors at Dinosaur Provincial Park. They sit in a circle around the remains of a smaller turtle. Every summer, visitors come to this park in western Canada to see the bones of ancient creatures. Tanke is a paleontologist, a scientist who studies animals and plants that lived long ago. He uses the brush, chisel, and other tools in front of him to dig up the remains of dinosaurs and other creatures. He keeps a record in his notebook of what he finds. Scientists have recovered as many as 200,000 dinosaur bones from this park during the past hundred years. They have found about 300 skeletons — many of them complete.

Although dinosaurs died out millions of years ago, they didn't completely disappear. In some places, their bones survive. One such place is Dinosaur Provincial Park. It lies in the western part of Canada, near Calgary, Alberta. There, people have found more dinosaur bones than in any other place on earth. They also have found the bones of more kinds of dinosaurs — 30 kinds in all.

When dinosaurs roamed this area, the climate was different. It was as warm as Florida is now. The climate made the area a perfect place for dinosaurs. Scientists think that is why so many kinds lived in what is now Dinosaur Provincial Park.

About 65 million years ago, scientists believe, all the dinosaurs in the world died out. The scientists aren't sure why. Over a long period of time, several things happened to preserve their bones in the park area. First, river mud containing sand, minerals, and dead plant matter buried the dinosaur bones. The wet mud kept them from decaying. Gradually, minerals replaced the soft parts of the bones. A shallow sea later covered the mud and bones. After millions of years, the sea dried up. The mud hardened into rock. The land shifted and parts of it tilted. A long, rocky ridge pushed upward. These changes brought the buried bones close to the surface of the earth.

Scientists discovered the first of these bones about a hundred years ago. They have uncovered thousands more since then. The bones give the scientists valuable information about life long ago.

PAUL VON BAICH (ABOVE AND OPPOSITE)

This painting shows the skeleton of a horned dinosaur called Chasmosaurus (kaz-moh-SAWR-us). Chasmosaurus was about the size of a present-day rhinoceros. A smaller dinosaur, the doglike Dromaeosaurus *(droh-mee-oh-SAWR-us), searches among the bones for food. Scientists found the remains of both these creatures in Dinosaur Provincial Park.*

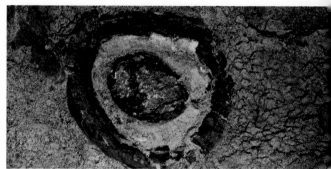

Part of a dinosaur leg bone pokes out of the ground in Dinosaur Provincial Park. This bone is about 6 inches across (15 cm). Its end has been broken off, revealing the inside structure. Minerals in water that once covered the area darkened the outer part of the bone. The inner part of the bone is lighter. Hardened mud fills its hollow center. Layers of ancient mud that gradually became soft stone form the striped hills of the park (left). The layers contain preserved bones from many different periods of time. Rain and melting snow carved grooves in the hills.

69

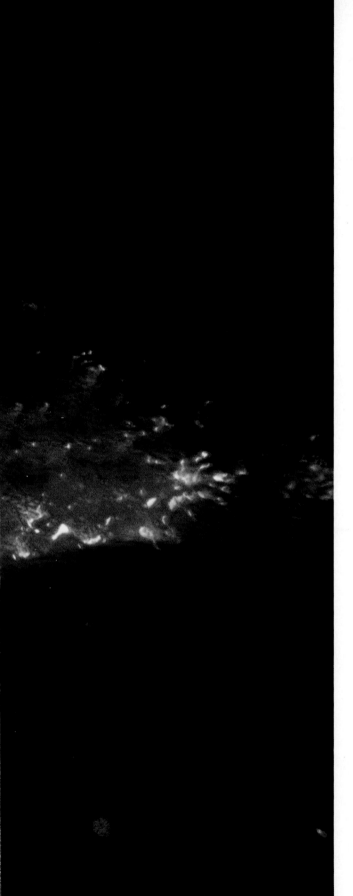

Fantastic Faces

If you were to design a really weird-looking fish face, it might not be any more unusual than the faces of a lot of living sea creatures. Many fish have features that seem odd to humans. Yet these features often serve useful purposes. By studying the faces of some fish, you can tell a lot about them.

A face may give clues to where a fish lives. Strange shapes or colors may serve as camouflage (KAM-uh-flazh). They help the fish blend in with its surroundings. Camouflage gives a fish protection. Enemies might mistake the camouflaged fish for leaves, rocks, seaweed — or even for other kinds of animals. You can often guess where a fish lives by the things it seems to match. For example, a sand-colored fish probably spends its time on the sandy seafloor.

A brightly colored face may serve a different purpose. It may help the fish advertise itself. A recognizable color pattern makes it easy for a fish to find others of the same kind. Bright colors on the face may also help protect a fish. Some colorful fish taste bad. A few can even be poisonous. Their colors may warn other fish to stay away.

Some fish use a spine on the forehead to attract food. This spine looks somewhat like a fishing rod with bait on the end. When smaller fish swim up to investigate the bait, the smaller fish often become dinner.

On these and the next pages, you'll see several fantastic-looking fish faces. Before you read about each fish, try to guess something about it from its face.

This fierce-looking face belongs to a gentle creature called a batfish (left). It seldom swims. Instead, it stands or moves along the seafloor on its fins. It travels so slowly that a person can catch it by hand. You can't see it here, but the batfish has a built-in fishing pole, complete with bait. The pole lies hidden in a small tube above the fish's eyes. When the batfish gets hungry, it pushes the pole out and twists it. A knob of flesh on the end jiggles like bait. The lure attracts smaller fish, which the batfish eats. Batfish live in both deep and shallow waters in many parts of the world.

GERI MURPHY

Where's the deer-crossing sign? What looks like antlers on the head of this small fish (left) are really growths of flesh called cirri (SEAR-eye). The cirri help the fish blend with the surrounding sea plants, corals, and jagged rocks. This fish is a yellowfin fringehead. It belongs to a group of fish called blennies. Many kinds of blennies have cirri on their heads. Blennies usually are small fish. Most kinds grow only a few inches long. They spend most of their time hiding in shells, in holes dug by other animals, or in old bottles. Blennies rarely swim. Most leave their hiding places only to feed on tiny plants and animals, to mate, and to lay eggs. Blennies live in warm waters in all parts of the world. Yellowfin fringeheads live only on rocky reefs off the coast of California.

HOWARD HALL (OPPOSITE)

Can you see why the goosefish (right) is also called the allmouth? The mouth of a goosefish is often as large as a dinner plate. Its appetite matches its mouth. The goosefish eats almost anything. Its diet includes small sharks, squid, crabs, other fish, and even diving birds. It grabs passing meals with needle-sharp teeth. Some goosefish weigh as much as 100 pounds (45 kg) and grow as long as 5 feet ($1^1/_2$ m). The growths that look like weeds under the mouth are bits of skin. They help camouflage the fish when it rests among seaweed on the ocean floor. Goosefish live in most oceans of the world.

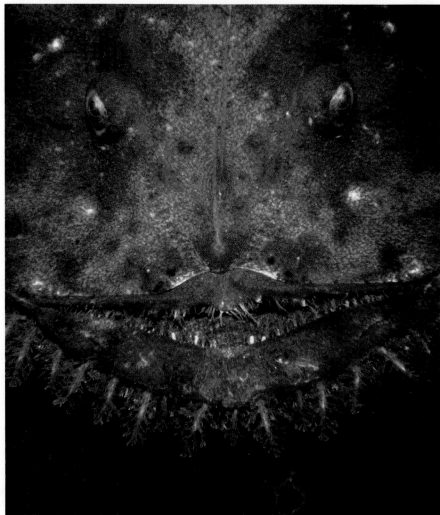

DOUGLAS FAULKNER/SALLY FAULKNER COLLECTION

You might say that the psychedelic fish (sye-kuh-DELL-ick) has good looks and bad taste (left). The brightly colored creature belongs to a group of fish called dragonets. The group includes some of the most brilliantly colored fish in the world. Mucus that covers the body of the psychedelic may taste bad to other fish. Some experts believe the psychedelic's bright colors warn other creatures not to take a taste. Psychedelic fish live in warm coastal waters off the Philippine Islands and off northern Australia. They spend most of their time on the seafloor and hide by burying themselves in the sand. Psychedelic fish grow about 3 inches long (8 cm).

TOM MYERS

73

Twins: A Double Mystery

Identical twins have more in common than their looks. Even those raised apart may lead remarkably similar lives. Often they choose the same clothes. They have the same fears and problems. They work at the same kinds of jobs. They give their children similar names. They get sick at the same time and have the same kinds of diseases. Sometimes one twin seems to be able to feel the pain of the other — or to sense when the other twin is in trouble.

Scientists don't know why identical twins are so much alike in their behavior. But they are trying to find out. Their studies have

Mirrors multiply Wendy and Patty Determan into a roomful of look-alikes (above). The Determan sisters are identical twins. So are about 25 million other people. "It's fun to grow up with someone who is going through exactly the same things you are," says Wendy. "Patty is more than a sister. She's my best friend. Each of us usually knows what the other is thinking." Most people can't tell Patty and Wendy apart, unless they get to know them very well. In school, the twins often enjoyed playing tricks on their teachers and classmates. "Every April Fool's Day, we'd change places in class," says Patty. The 19-year-old girls live in Fairfield, Connecticut.

AL SATTERWHITE

caused them to take a new look at the old question of what is learned and what is inherited.

One out of every 90 births produces twins. One-quarter of these are identical. The rest are fraternal twins. Fraternal twins are born when two separately fertilized eggs grow inside the mother at the same time. Such twins look no more alike than any other brothers or sisters. Identical twins grow from one fertilized egg that splits in two. As a result, the twins inherit the same sex and the same physical characteristics.

What other identical characteristics do they inherit? That's what scientists are trying to find out.

An identical twin named Terry Connolly breathes into a machine that tests her lungs (above). Later, she and her twin, Margaret Richardson, look through their baby pictures, while psychologist Thomas Bouchard asks them questions (left). Terry lives in Bolton, England. Margaret lives in Nottingham, England. The sisters took part in a study of identical twins who had been adopted as infants by different families. Scientists at the University of Minnesota performed medical tests on such twins and asked each of them 15,000 questions. The scientists discovered many similarities in the twins' lives. Twins named Jim had married women named Betty. Both Jims owned dogs named Toy, vacationed at the beach, and worked as deputy sheriffs.

Virginia and Grace Kennedy, identical twins from San Diego, California, talk in their own language (right). Like some other twins, they invented a language no one else could understand. Most twins forget their special language as they learn regular words. The Kennedy twins didn't forget it. They spoke in a mixture of mispronounced English and German. Both languages were spoken in their home. Mispronouncing words so badly that they sound like another language is called idioglossia (id-ee-uh-GLAH-see-uh). It's common among twins. They are together so much that they copy each other's mistakes. Because they are so much alike, they don't need many words to communicate with each other. Now 11, Virginia and Grace have learned to speak normal English.

Heavenly Sights

Sunlight plus water can add up to heavenly sights. You certainly have seen one — a rainbow. Rainbows form when sunlight passes through raindrops. The water bends the light rays, making a pattern of colors.

Ice crystals in clouds sometimes bend light and create patterns, too. If the crystals point in many directions, the result is a halo — a ring of light around the sun. If rod-shaped crystals lie parallel to the ground, they may produce a bright curve of light above the sun. The curve is called an upper tangent arc. If the rod-shaped crystals stand on end, you may see bright spots on either side of the sun. People call the spots mock suns.

Rise and shine. At dawn in Massachusetts, ice crystals in the cold upper air produce an unusual combination of patterns (above). The picture shows a tangent arc, a mock sun, and a halo. The tangent arc is the curve of light near the top of the picture. The small bright spot at the left is the mock sun. This spot is bright like the sun but much smaller. You can see the sun faintly on the horizon. The halo forms a large circle around the sun. Halos appear more often than other heavenly sights. You are more likely to spot a halo than a rainbow. If you see a halo, try to move into the shade while you look at it. That way, you'll see it more clearly. Looking at a halo won't hurt your eyes, but be sure to look only at the halo, not at the sun. You should never look directly at the sun!

DENNIS DI CICCO/SKY & TELESCOPE

Hidden Lives

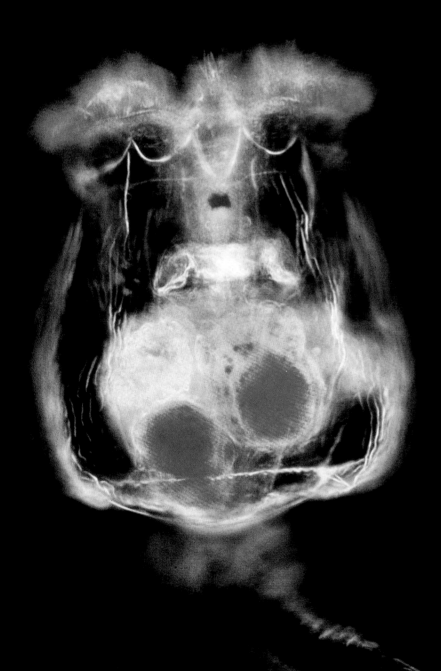

If you lost your canteen in the desert, you wouldn't survive very long. Without water, you'd live only a few days. Your body needs water to carry out all the processes of life, from turning food into energy to getting rid of wastes. Some living things, however, can get along without water for years and years.

If you take away all traces of water from many seeds, from some bacteria, and from a wide variety of microscopic animals, they dry up and appear to be dead. These seeds, bacteria, and animals can lie shriveled up for long periods. Although they show no signs of life, they are not dead. All are in a state called cryptobiosis (krip-toe-by-OH-sis). As soon as water is added, they swell up, start to uncurl, and burst with life!

The word "cryptobiosis" means "hidden life." During this state, the normal activities of living come to a halt. Cryptobiosis has puzzled people for more than two centuries. In 1702, a Dutch scientist named Anton Van Leeuwenhoek discovered that certain tiny animals could "play dead" and then come back to life. He made the discovery while looking through a microscope.

Since then, scientists have studied certain animals and plants, trying to unlock the secrets of their hidden lives. The scientists leave the animals and plants in a dried-up state for long periods of time. Then they put water on them. Presto! Life picks up where it left off. Seeds sprout, eggs hatch, and small animals move about once more.

This microscopic animal is no wider than a strand of hair. But it has an ability most larger animals lack. When deprived of water, it dries up and appears to be dead. It shows signs of life as soon as water is added to it. The animal is called a rotifer (ROE-tih-fur). It lives in ponds, puddles, and other still or slow-moving waters. It eats small plants that sometimes form green scum on the surface. This rotifer was photographed through a microscope. It is shown more than 500 times its normal size.

Drop by drop, Dr. James Clegg adds water to the eggs of brine shrimp (right). Dr. Clegg, a biologist at the University of Miami, in Florida, is one of the scientists who study brine shrimp and other small creatures that can survive for long periods in a dried-up state. This state is called cryptobiosis (krip-toe-by-OH-sis). Dried brine-shrimp eggs can sit for years in such a state. When moistened, the eggs hatch, and active brine shrimp emerge.

Dried brine-shrimp eggs lie piled in test tubes (below). The tiny eggs are shown twice life size. Dr. Clegg keeps thousands of these eggs for his experiments. The eggs and newly hatched brine shrimp are commonly sold in pet stores. People feed the shrimp to tropical fish. Brine-shrimp eggs can stay bottled up on store shelves for months. When the eggs are placed in salt water, they hatch into live brine shrimp.

HENRY GROSKINSKY ©1980 (ALL)

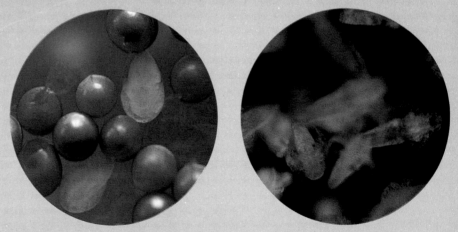

After seven years in a dried-up state, brine-shrimp eggs gradually come alive. The pictures above show the eggs as they hatch. The pictures were made through a microscope. Both the eggs and the brine shrimp are shown 75 times life size. When someone adds water to the eggs, it takes about three hours for them to swell up to their original size. They begin to hatch about nine hours later (above, left). Finally, fully hatched, wriggling brine shrimp start swimming around in the water (above, right). The entire hatching process, from dried-up eggs to the live shrimp you see here, takes about 24 hours.

ROBERT O. SCHUSTER (ALL)

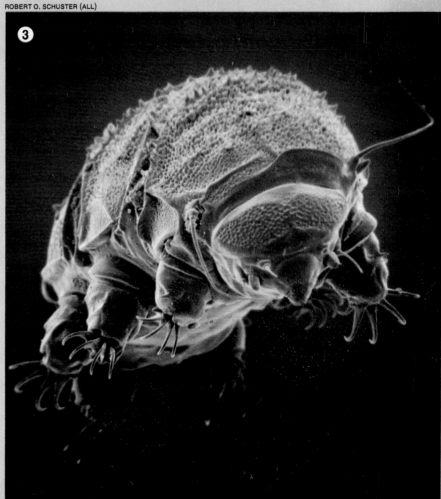

Like a creature from a monster movie, this weird-looking animal slowly awakens. It claws the air, then creeps forward. It's a tardigrade (TAR-dih-grade), a tiny, slow-moving creature that lives in ponds or in moist soil. Although the tardigrade looks large here, you could not see it without using a microscope. These pictures were taken by a special kind of microscope that does not make color pictures.

(1) In a state of cryptobiosis, the tardigrade has curled up tightly into a barrel shape. It appears to be dead. There is almost no water in the animal's body now. Normally, water would make up about 85 percent of its body weight. This picture shows the tardigrade 600 times life size.

(2) As the tardigrade is moistened, it slowly uncurls. It begins to extend its claws, which had been drawn into its body. Here the tardigrade is shown 750 times life size.

(3) Uncurled and fully awake, the tardigrade begins to move around and search for food. Its body has filled out to normal size. The animal is shown 600 times larger than life size.

Tardigrades and rotifers probably hold the animal record for spending the longest time in a cryptobiotic state. Some have been revived after more than a hundred years.

Twenty-nine Days Hath September

1 In ancient Rome, the month of September was the seventh month of the year, and a year had 10 months instead of 12. Each month had 29 days — the time between one new moon and the next. The first day of the month was new moon day, the day for money lenders to collect.

2 The Latin word for moon is *luna,* so people call this division of days a lunar calendar. The month of Martius (now called March) was the first month of the Roman year. December was the last month of the year.

3 The lunar calendar had one big problem. It didn't match the seasons. The moon has nothing to do with the change of seasons. The seasons change as the earth tilts on its axis while revolving around the sun.

7 After the year of confusion, the Roman ruler asked an Egyptian astronomer to make the Roman calendar work as well as Egypt's. The astronomer suggested adding extra days to the months so that each year would have $365\frac{1}{4}$ days. You can't divide $365\frac{1}{4}$ by 12 and get an even number of days. The astronomer worked things out by changing the number of days in some months.

8 Soon after the days were added, two months got new names. Julius Caesar was the Roman ruler who put the new calendar into effect. A month in the new calendar was named for him. The month of Quintilis became Julius (now July). Julius was a long month. It had 31 days.

9 The next ruler, Augustus Caesar, had a month named for him, too. The old Sextilis became Augustus (now August). It also got 31 days. Sextilis had been a 30-day month, so the extra day had to come from some other month. It was taken from the shortest month — February. Now February usually had 28 days. In leap year, it had 29. All went well for about 800 years, until someone noticed a small mistake the Romans had made.

4   Each season lasts 91 days, plus a few hours. That adds up to about 365¼ days a year. But the Roman lunar calendar contained only 290 days a year. This mismatch caused a lot of strange things to happen. Seasonal festivals often came at the wrong time of year. Can you imagine having a harvest festival at planting time or a spring festival in winter? With a calendar that was out of step with the seasons, that could happen.

5   Finally, the Roman rulers decided to change the calendar. They gave it 12 months instead of 10. To make the change, they added two months between the last month of one year (December) and the first month of the next year (Martius). They named one new month Januarius. They named the other Februarius.

6   The 12-month calendar was better, but it still wasn't quite right. Each month still had only 29 days in it. So each year had 348 days, instead of 365¼. To keep the calendar in step with the seasons, Roman rulers had to add an extra month from time to time. Sometimes the rulers forgot to do this at the right time. Then they would have to catch up. In one year—47 B.C.—three extra months were added. Some people called that year "the year of confusion."

10 A monk spotted the calendar error in A.D. 730. He figured out that the year did not have exactly 365¼ days in it, after all. The year really contained 365¼ days *minus* 11 minutes and 14 seconds. Eventually, those extra minutes and seconds added up to extra days. In 730, the calendar was 5½ days ahead of the seasons. The monk tried to get something done, but nobody listened. Finally, after another 800 years passed . . .

11 . . . the Pope in Rome was reminded of the problem. Easter was coming later every year. Every date on the calendar was being pushed farther into the year. To correct things, the Pope shortened the month of September 1582 by ten days. Now the calendar matched the seasons. The Pope decreed that, in the future, only one out of every four centuries should begin with a leap year. That would subtract three days from the calendar every 400 years.

12 Catholic countries in Europe obeyed the Pope and changed their calendars at once. Most Protestant countries did not. The American colonies held out until 1752. By that time, they had 11 extra days. Finally, the colonies dropped 11 days and began using the new calendar. Birthdays and holidays changed. George Washington was born on February 11. But when the calendar changed, his birthday came on February 22, where it is today.

Lasers: 'Magic' Lights

A beam of light moves across a diamond, the hardest substance on earth. Crack! The diamond splits. A beam of light strikes a thin steel needle. Zap! The light drills a hole through the needle. A beam of light touches a wart. Sssssssss. Heat from the light burns off the wart painlessly. It vanishes in a puff of smoke.

A beam of light that can do all these things, and many more, seems like a magic ray in a science-fiction movie. This amazing tool is called a laser beam.

Laser beams have much more power than ordinary light beams. In ordinary light beams, tiny particles called photons (FOH-tahns) travel in many directions. When you turn on a flashlight, you may notice that the beam of light spreads, fades, and disappears a short distance from where you are standing. That happens because the paths of the photons quickly spread apart.

In laser beams, the photons all travel in a straight line. So laser beams are very strong, and they can travel much farther than

instruments that control the way the photons in the light beam move. Scientists use many kinds of materials to make laser beams. The beams may be different in color and have different characteristics, depending on the materials used. The power of a beam can be adjusted. Scientists tailor each laser beam to the job it will do.

The list of jobs is long — and growing. Surgeons use laser light to make delicate cuts. The heat from the beam seals blood vessels as it cuts, making operations almost bloodless. Manufacturers use laser beams for cutting and welding metal. Scientists use them to send signals into space and to measure distances to other planets. Lasers do a variety of everyday tasks, too. They scan groceries for price codes at the checkout counter. They measure air pollution. The "magic" lights have so many uses that scientists think every home may have a laser someday.

just that. The laser beam is aimed so that it is parallel to the ground. By following the beam, the scraper can make a field perfectly flat. A tractor pulls the scraper, which smooths out the earth. The field will be used for farming. Leveling it will keep water from running off. This can save about a third of the water normally used for irrigation. The red coloring of this laser beam makes it easy to see and follow. People also use colored laser beams to guide construction machines that must follow a straight line for a long distance.

H. EDWARD KIM, N.G.S.

Light explodes against a dark background (above). As taped music plays, the light may grow, shrink, or change shape. It may turn into a streak, a swirl, or a dot. It may sway, skip, or leap in rhythm with the music. A computer and a technician called a laserist control this colorful show, known as Laserium. Many museums and observatories now put on similar laser-light shows. Some rock musicians use laser lights to produce special effects in their shows.

LASER EFFECT BY LASERIUM/LASER IMAGES, INC.

Laser beams enable Dr. Joseph J. Barrett to analyze a gas sample (left). Dr. Barrett is a physicist with Allied Corporation, in New Jersey. Here, he aims two laser beams of different colors at a metal container. The container holds a mixture of gases. By adjusting the color of one of the beams, Dr. Barrett can tell what gases are in the container and how much of each one is present. Scientists use this method to analyze chemicals and to measure air pollution.

THE IMAGE BANK/WILLIAM RIVELLI

Jewel thieves, beware! Diamonds can now be "fingerprinted." Charles W. Jahraus, of Chicago, Illinois, beams laser light onto a gem through a hole in Polaroid film (above). The pattern in the diamond shows up on the film. Diamonds are crystals. Like all crystals, they form patterns. No two diamonds have exactly the same pattern, just as no two snow crystals do. The pattern of a diamond crystal cannot be seen with the unaided eye. But laser light reveals it and records it on film. The print can help a diamond owner identify and recover a stolen gem — even if it has been cut into a different shape.

FRED WARD/BLACK STAR

Want to change a scene? Laser light can help you do it. This picture of skaters in action (left) started out as an ordinary color slide. A laser beam and a computer, working together, changed it. A weak laser beam scanned the photograph and translated its colors and shapes into electronic signals. The signals went into a computer. It read them and formed a picture on a video-display terminal. By changing instructions to the computer, an operator can change the appearance of the picture. Laser scanners have many uses in the printing industry. They helped produce the color pictures in this book.

JO ANNE KALISH/JOE DI MAGGIO/LUMIERE

Brushing Up on Teeth

Brushing an elephant's teeth is a giant job. Each tooth can grow almost as big and as heavy as a brick. An elephant in Sri Lanka is getting its teeth cleaned by its handler (below). He uses a coconut husk. It has a rough surface like a scouring pad. The elephant has only eight working teeth. As each one wears out, an unused tooth from the back of the mouth pushes forward. An elephant uses 48 teeth during its lifetime. Chewing about 300 pounds (136 kg) of plant material every day grinds down its teeth. When the last set of teeth wears out, the elephant can no longer chew. Unable to eat, it dies.

GILBERT M. GROSVENOR

The toothbrush wasn't invented until about 500 years ago, but people cleaned their teeth long before that. They used a wide variety of materials.

In India, they scrubbed their teeth with small roots from the arak tree. Many people in Africa, India, and Asia still use such roots. They chew one end of a piece of root. This softens it and makes it into a kind of brush. The wood of the arak tree contains a substance that whitens teeth and kills germs.

Citizens of ancient Greece rubbed mint on their teeth to sweeten their breath. Romans wiped their teeth with a sponge or a cloth dipped in a honey mixture.

Certain animals, such as monkeys and apes, also practice good dental habits. They regularly pick their teeth with twigs. Many zoo animals have their teeth cleaned and checked as part of their regular health care. More and more people are cleaning their pets' teeth or having their veterinarians do it. To brush up on other facts about dental care, read on.

When George Washington was President of the United States, he had the teeth of his horses picked and cleaned every day (below). He wanted the six white horses that pulled his presidential coach to look their best at all times. Regular tooth cleaning benefits horses, just as it does humans. Horses with bad teeth cannot chew food properly. Cleaning their teeth helps prevent cavities and gum disease.

GERRY YEALDHALL/EUCALYPTUS TREE STUDIO

RICHARD WALDRYS/EUCALYPTUS TREE STUDIO

ANIMALS ANIMALS/BRADLEY SMITH

Open wide! A killer whale shows its teeth (above). Having its teeth brushed is part of the killer whale's act at Sea World in San Diego, California. The whale even rinses its mouth. When the trainer has finished the cleanup, he puts his head into the killer whale's mouth. That's part of the act, too. In the wild, a killer whale uses its sharp, pointed teeth to catch and tear apart prey. The whale does not chew its food. It swallows big bites whole.

When the French emperor Napoleon Bonaparte went to war, he didn't neglect his teeth. Even on the battlefield, he brushed with a gold-handled toothbrush fit for an emperor (above). His wife, Marie Louise, had the toothbrush specially made for Napoleon to take on his campaign to Russia in 1812. Napoleon wasn't the only person who brushed in style at that time. Many wealthy people in Europe used toothbrushes with silver or ivory handles. Most people used toothbrushes with ox-bone handles. No matter what kind of handle a toothbrush had, it usually had bristles of cow or hog hair. Toothbrush makers continued to use natural bristles until about the middle of this century. They imported the hair from China. During World War II, when natural bristles were hard to get, manufacturers switched to nylon bristles. That is what most of us brush with today.

Are two heads better than one? Some people think so. A new kind of toothbrush (above) cleans the front and back sides of the teeth at the same time. Proper brushing removes plaque (PLAK), a substance that builds up on teeth and causes cavities. How can you tell if you're brushing properly? Another far-out toothbrush may help you. It contains musical chimes. When the chimes jingle, the brushing action is right.

ARTHUR IDDINGS

Arctic Adventure

Across 500 miles of ice (805 km), Japanese adventurer Naomi Uemura treks toward the North Pole. Naomi's only companions on the journey were dogs. They pulled his sled loaded with supplies. To protect his body from bitter arctic cold, Naomi wore clothes made from polar-bear skin. Once, a polar bear raided his camp. The powerful beast ate some of Naomi's food. It nudged him through the wall of his tent. Then it went away.

Naomi traveled over huge plates of shifting ice that float on the surface of the Arctic Ocean. Sometimes the ice would crack open with a frightening bang. Often, Naomi had to cut through ridges of ice that blocked his way. He saw some ridges that were as high as a three-story building.

When he reached his goal, after 55 days, Naomi was a happy man (small picture). He had fulfilled a dream. Many explorers had traveled to the North Pole before him, including Robert E. Peary with his famous expedition of 1909. But in 1978, Naomi became the first person ever to reach the pole alone.

A.D. 1

1982

1982

Three North Poles

Everyone knows that the North Pole isn't a pole sticking out of the ground. But few people realize that the earth has not one, not two, but *three* North Poles! None can be seen, and two of them are always moving. The three poles are shown on the map (above). The pole that never moves is called the geographic pole. It's shown in yellow. This pole marks the spot in the Arctic Ocean where the north-south lines on a globe meet. These imaginary lines, called lines of longitude, help people locate positions on charts, maps, and globes.

The magnetic North Pole is shown in red. It is about a thousand miles (1,609 km) south of the geographic North Pole. This is the area compass needles point to. The earth acts as if a powerful magnet runs through its core. The northern end of the core attracts the magnetized compass needle. The magnetic pole moves about 5 miles (8 km) a year because the earth's core is gradually shifting. The red line shows the path the magnetic pole has traveled during the past 2,000 years.

The third pole, shown in green, follows a similar path. At present, it lies about 500 miles (805 km) east of the magnetic pole. It is called the geomagnetic pole. It marks the area where the magnetic pole *would* lie if the earth had a magnetic bar running through its *exact* center. The instruments of satellites far out in space "see" the pole at a spot slightly different from its real location. Scientists who work with satellite information use the geomagnetic pole in their calculations.

If three North Poles aren't enough, there are three South Poles, too — for exactly the same reasons.

JAIME QUINTERO

Giant Sea Creatures

Giant creatures that live in the sea make animals living on land seem small. The largest ocean animal is the blue whale. It weighs 25 times as much as an elephant. Giant clams, giant octopuses, squids, fish, and sea worms all grow to huge sizes.

Big does not always mean bad where giants of the deep are concerned. Some large sea creatures have reputations they don't deserve. In old movies, for instance, a giant clam like the one at right might quickly clamp its shells around the feet of a deep-sea diver. The clam would threaten the diver's life. In real life, a clam never catches food — or anything else — in this manner. Its shells close very slowly.

The blue whale is a quiet, peaceable creature. It does not overturn ships. It does not bother swimmers. It ignores people and feeds only on tiny plants and animals.

Most sharks are not as dangerous as people think. Only 30 of the 250 kinds of sharks would ever attack humans.

Why do giant sea creatures grow so large? For one thing, the ocean is full of plant and animal life. There is enough food to satisfy even very big appetites. For another, giants that live in water do not have to depend on their bones and muscles for support. The water helps to support them.

Many sea creatures never stop growing, even when they reach adulthood. Some fish, lobsters, and jellyfish, for instance, get a little longer and a little broader every year.

You seldom see large sea creatures close to shore, but you might see one if you are out in a boat. Perhaps then a large whale will rise out of the water and slowly sink back, spouting all the while. Maybe a manta ray, a so-called "devilfish," will leap near you and disappear into the water again. Then, as a diver once said, you might "feel privileged to have been there."

This giant clam lies with its wavy pink shells open (right). It measures almost a foot across (30 cm). The clam never has to look for food. It gets most of its nourishment from tiny green plants that live in its soft body. The plants are called algae (AL-jee). Like all plants, algae need sunlight to grow. That is why the clam stays near the surface with its shells open. It also feeds on little plants and animals that drift into its open shells. Some giant clams grow to be 4 feet long (1 1/4 m) and weigh 500 pounds (227 kg).

DOUGLAS FAULKNER/SALLY FAULKNER COLLECTION

People call this animal a whale shark. It is the world's largest fish. A few kinds of whales may grow larger, but whales are not fish. They are mammals. Like other mammals, whales breathe air. The two divers swimming alongside the whale shark do not fear it. They know it will not attack them. Unlike some other sharks, whale sharks are gentle. They eat mostly tiny plants. They also eat small fish. Whale sharks may grow as long as 65 feet (20 m) and weigh as much as 25 tons (23 t). That's as much as 11 large cars weigh! Do you see the group of little fish swimming in front of this shark? Sailors named them pilot fish because they seem to lead the way. Their real reason for swimming near the shark's head is to snatch bits of food when the giant eats.

This diver hitches a ride on a whale shark's tail (right). The shark glides slowly through the water, gently waving its tail from side to side. It ignores its human passenger. Although many large sea creatures are gentle, amateur divers shouldn't try to take rides on them. A sudden move by an animal this large could cause serious injury to the diver.

"Strangest of all the fishes in the sea." That's what some experts call the ocean sunfish (right). It looks as if the rear half of its body is missing. Travelers named the ocean sunfish for its habit of floating near the surface. It often lies on its side and lets sea gulls pick off tiny animals that live on its skin. It is a big fish. The largest one ever found measured 13 feet high (4 m) and 11 feet long (3 m). Ocean sunfish eat jellyfish, a meal most sea creatures avoid. The sunfish have few enemies. Leathery skin helps keep them from being hurt.

Like a huge bat flying underwater, a manta ray takes a diver for a ride (below). Flexible projections at the sides of the manta ray's mouth help it draw in small fish. People once thought the projections looked like pictures of a devil's horns. They gave the manta ray the name "devilfish." Some people feared it. But manta rays are harmless to humans. Most are shy creatures. They won't let a person get this close. Some manta rays weigh almost 2 tons ($1^3/_4$ t) and measure 20 feet (6 m) from wing tip to wing tip. Do you see the "handlebars" the diver grasps? They are fish called remoras. Remoras attach themselves to larger fish by using the suction cups on their heads.

HOWARD HALL (BOTH)

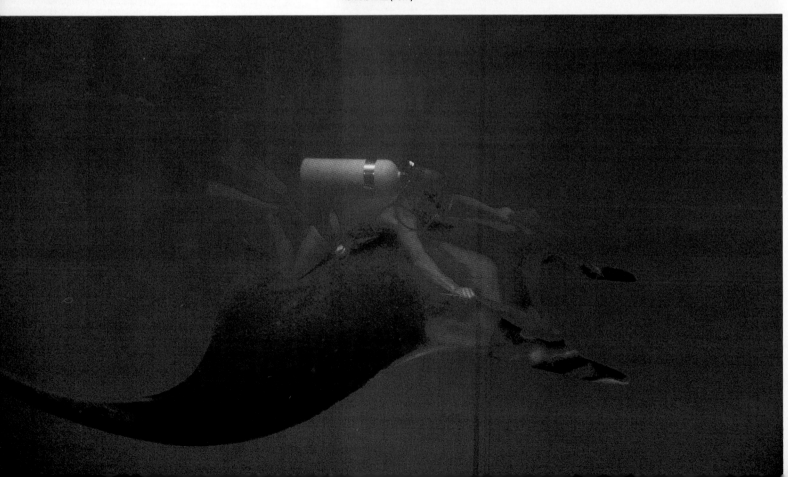

You may have seen jellyfish washed up on a beach, but you've probably never seen one as big as this anywhere. This kind of jellyfish may grow 20 feet long (6 m), from the top of its umbrella-shaped body to the tips of its tentacles. The umbrella resembles a clear plastic bag filled with jelly. The mouth lies on the underside of the umbrella. This jellyfish uses its poisonous tentacles to get food. It paralyzes passing fish by stinging them. Then it pulls the fish into its mouth and eats them. Some fish are not affected by the poison. They live right under the umbrella. This keeps them safe from their enemies.

JACK DRAFAHL/KRITTER LABS

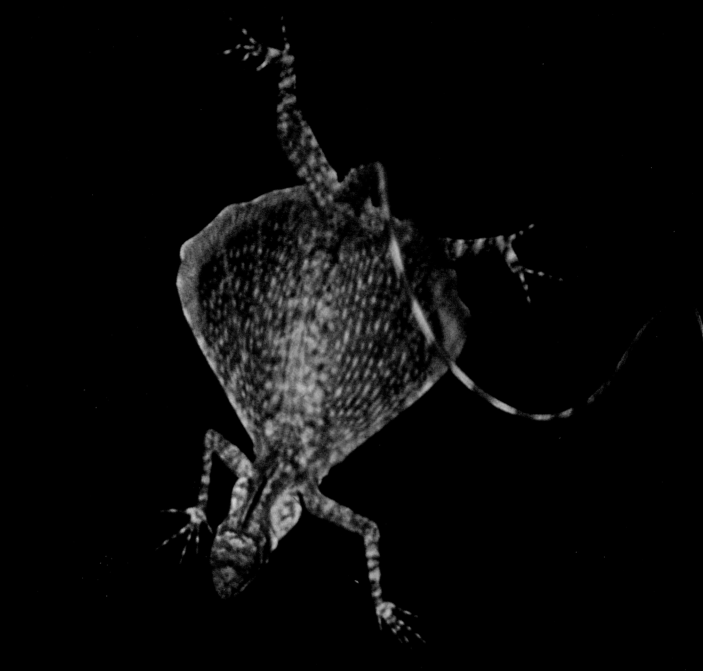

Animal Hang Gliders

Of all the animals in the world, only birds and bats can fly through the air. Right?

Wrong! Some other animals also "fly." They don't fly as birds do, by flapping wings. Instead they glide. Many travel surprisingly long distances. The animals shown on these pages all have loose or ribbed skin along the sides of their bodies. When they stretch out their legs and leap, the skin spreads wide, forming flaps. The flaps turn the animals into little hang gliders.

Animals that move through the air have advantages over earthbound creatures. They can flee from danger quickly. They can cover long distances in search of food or mates without using much energy. And what a view they must have!

Leaping lizard! This animal glides on ribbed "wings" of skin (above). Because of the brilliant coloring beneath its wings, some people call this creature the butterfly lizard. Others call it the flying dragon. Like all flying lizards, the flying dragon lives in forests in Southeast Asia. It uses its legs to climb trees. Then it glides from tree to tree or back to earth. When it folds its wings and sits motionless on a tree branch, the dull markings on its back blend with the branch. This leaping lizard grows from 12 to 16 inches long (30 to 41 cm), including the tail.

Coming in for a landing, a flying squirrel heads toward a branch (left). A flying squirrel always looks before it leaps. It selects a landing spot, stares at it, and leans to the right and to the left. Scientists think these motions help the animal judge how far it must glide. Finally the squirrel springs. It spreads out skin flaps that reach from its front legs to its hind legs. Flying squirrels live in many parts of the world, including North America. The smallest are no bigger than a mouse. The largest are 3 feet long (1 m) from nose to tail tip. Some big flying squirrels can glide as far as a quarter of a mile. If you have never spotted a flying squirrel, there's a good reason. The animals usually sleep by day. They do most of their flying in darkness.

Pilot and passenger rest before takeoff. A baby flying lemur clings to its mother as she hangs from a branch (right). She grips the branch with the claws of her front feet. Her baby snuggles into furry skin that stretches from the tip of her front feet to the end of her tail. When the mother flying lemur is at rest, this loose skin forms a furry cape for the baby. As the mother takes off, the skin spreads out. The baby uses its tiny, sharp claws to cling to the fur of its mother's belly while she is in the air. A flying lemur steers by leaning from side to side. It brakes by lifting its tail and lands with its head up. When a baby grows too heavy to ride along, it must learn to glide by itself. It practices with its mother until it can keep up with her. A full-grown flying lemur can glide as far as 450 feet (137 m). Flying lemurs grow to about the size of house cats. They live in the forests of Malaysia, a country in Southeast Asia. Flying lemurs, like other gliding animals, can fly from tree to tree or from treetop to ground. But they cannot fly upward. To climb, they must use their feet.

Soaring on Sun Power

Up, up, and away goes an unusual aircraft called the *Solar Challenger*. It is made of lightweight plastic. On July 7, 1981, it cruised above farmlands and a choppy body of water at a not-very-fast 30 miles an hour (48 km/h). When it landed, 5½ hours and 163 miles (262 km) later, it made history.

On this flight, as on all its flights, the *Solar Challenger* used no fuel. This airplane flies on sun power alone. Its inventor, Dr. Paul MacCready, had to wait a month to arrange this flight because of cloudy weather. Other experimental planes have flown short distances using solar energy stored in batteries. But this plane carries no batteries. It depends on direct sunlight.

In 1981, the *Challenger* flew from an airport near Paris, France, to the southeast tip of England. It wasn't Dr. MacCready's first experimental plane to cross the English Channel or his first to take off without using fuel. Dr. MacCready, a California physicist and airplane designer, made news in 1977 with the *Gossamer*

The sun provides all the power the Solar Challenger *needs (above). Solar cells on the plane's wings and tail absorb energy from the sun's rays. The cells turn the energy into electricity that runs a small motor. The motor spins the* Challenger's *propeller. Builders work on the cockpit of this experimental craft as it takes shape in a California factory (below). Made of lightweight, extra-strong plastic, the Solar Challenger weighs only 210 pounds (95 kg). That's about as much as a large man. Dr. Paul MacCready designed the* Challenger *to show that solar cells can harness the sun's energy and use it to fly a plane.*

DRAYTON HAWKINS, N.G.S.

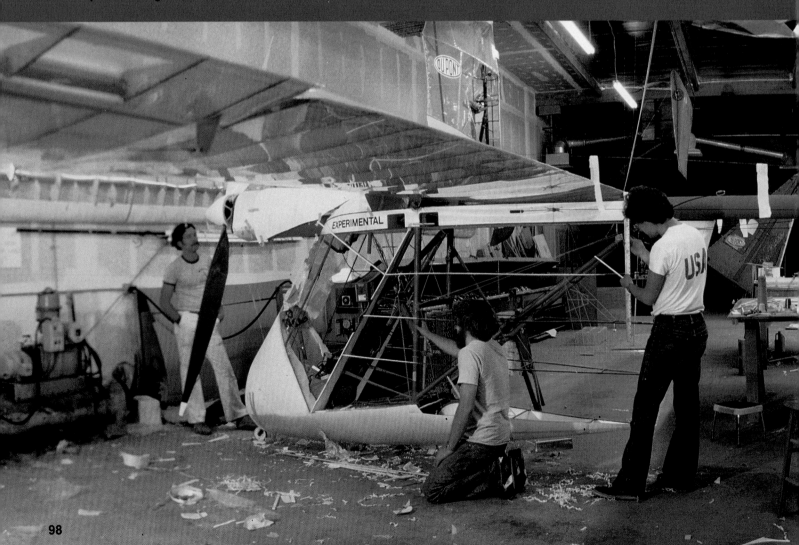

Before takeoff, crew members clean solar cells on the Challenger's wings (left). Moments later, the plane began its 1981 trip from France to England. Cleaning the cells before each takeoff is important. Even a thin coating of dust can cause them to produce less energy. More than 16,000 solar cells cover the Challenger's wings and tail. Engineers have put similar cells on space satellites. The cells gather energy to produce electricity while a spacecraft is in orbit.

Condor. That plane won an international prize by staying in the air for 7½ minutes on human energy. A pedaling bicyclist provided the power. Two years later, the *Gossamer Albatross* crossed the Channel in 2 hours and 49 minutes on pedal power. Then came the *Solar Challenger* and its successful sun-powered flight.

Will the flight of the *Challenger* change the way commercial airplanes fly? Dr. MacCready doesn't think so. "There's nothing practical about this design," he says. He built the plane to make people think more about new kinds of energy – and, of course, to prove that it could be done.

On a summer day, the Solar Challenger *crosses the English Channel. Most of the 1981 flight took place above the clouds, at an altitude of 11,000 feet (3,353 m). When clouds block the sun, the* Challenger *loses altitude gradually. Fortunately, the plane was in direct sunlight during most of this flight.*

"I made it!" Pilot Steve Ptacek gives the thumbs-up sign after his flight from France to England in the Challenger. The trip took 5$\frac{1}{2}$ hours, at an average speed of 30 miles an hour (48 km/h). "The view was superb," says Ptacek.

RANDA BISHOP/CONTACT

Test pilot Janice Brown prepares for a flight (below). "During takeoff," she says, "the Challenger feels like a butterfly struggling to leave the earth." Janice has flown the Challenger more often and taken it higher than anyone else—to 14,000 feet (4,267 m).

KEN ROGERS/BLACK STAR

Index

Bold type refers to illustrations; regular type refers to text.

CONSULTANTS

Suzanne F. Clewell, Ph.D., University of Maryland; Patricia Leadbetter King, National Cathedral School; Glenn O. Blough, LL.D., University of Maryland — *Educational Consultants*

Nicholas J. Long, Ph.D., University of Michigan — *Consulting Psychologist*

The Special Publications and School Services Division is grateful to the individuals, organizations, and agencies named or quoted within the text and the individuals cited here for their generous assistance:

Action Hygiene Products, Inc.
Alice Alldredge, University of California at Santa Barbara
Joseph Barrett, Allied Corporation
Pat Belth, Peekskill Area Health Center
Jean-Jacques Boisard, Parc Zoologique de Thoiry
Thomas Bouchard, University of Minnesota
Bill Brand, Sarah Lawrence College
Ralph Brauer, Institute for Marine Biomedical Research
Robert L. Christianson, U. S. Geological Survey
James P. Clegg, University of Miami
Phil Currie, Provincial Museum of Alberta
G. D. Dailley, African Lion Safari, Ontario
G. D. Dailley, Jr., African Lion Safari, Ontario
Clyde Davis, Marriott Corporation
Lewis Deitz, North Carolina State University
Dennis di Cicco, *Sky and Telescope*
Jim Doar, Boeing Computer Services
Art Durinsky, Information International
Embassies of Denmark, Greece, Italy, Japan, Mexico, Sweden, the Federal Republic of Germany, and the People's Republic of China; the British Embassy, the Korean Embassy, the Royal Netherlands Embassy, the Royal Thai Embassy
Steven Fuller, Yellowstone National Park
Michael Hackenberger, African Lion Safari, Ontario

Wayne Hamilton, Yellowstone National Park
Steven Hill, University of Maryland
Nicholas Hotton, Smithsonian Institution
Rick Hutchinson, Yellowstone National Park
Herbert Levi, Museum of Comparative Zoology
Bonnie Livingston, National Museum of Natural Sciences
Ron Lorentzen, U. S. Naval Oceanographic Office
Paul MacCready, AeroVironment
Eric G. Marason, Spectra-Physics
Kevin McCaffrey, Hewlett-Packard Computer Products
John E. McCosker, Steinhart Aquarium, Academy of Sciences
Michael W. Melvill, Rutan Aircraft Factory, Inc.
Mount Vernon Ladies' Association
Douglas Nelms, British Aerospace
Paul Opler, Fish and Wildlife Service, U. S. Department of Interior
Lee Perrizo, Fond du Lac Skyport
John Randall, Bishop Museum
Miles Roberts, National Zoological Park
W. O. Roberts, National Center for Atmospheric Research
Ray Robinson, U. S. Department of Commerce
A. I. Root Company
Edward S. Ross, California Academy of Sciences
Burt Rutan, Rutan Aircraft Factory, Inc.
Raymond Schar, U. S. Department of Agriculture
Sea World
C. C. Shuman, Bureau of Marine Resource Regulation and Development
Otmar Silberstein, McCormick & Co., Inc.
Victor Springer, Smithsonian Institution
John Stephens, Occidental College
Richard W. Thorington, Jr., Smithsonian Institution
Frank Waites, U. S. Naval Oceanographic Office
William Wallner, U. S. Forest Service Insect and Disease Laboratory
George E. Watson, Smithsonian Institution
David Wise, University of California, Irvine
T. K. Wood, University of Delaware

Library of Congress CIP Data
Main entry under title:

More far-out facts.

(Books for world explorers)
Includes index.
SUMMARY: Presents unusual facts about a wide range of topics, including plants, animals, food, earth sciences, and computers.
1. Science—Miscellanea—Juvenile literature.
[1. Science—Miscellanea]   I. National Geographic Society (U.S.)
II. Series.
Q163.M86   1982   031'.02   80-8798
ISBN 0-87044-384-4 (regular binding)   AACR2
ISBN 0-87044-389-5 (library binding)

PUBLISHED BY
THE NATIONAL GEOGRAPHIC SOCIETY
WASHINGTON, D. C.

Gilbert M. Grosvenor, *President*
Melvin M. Payne, *Chairman of the Board*
Owen R. Anderson, *Executive Vice President*
Robert L. Breeden, *Vice President, Publications and Educational Media*

PREPARED BY THE SPECIAL PUBLICATIONS AND SCHOOL SERVICES DIVISION

Donald J. Crump, *Director*
Philip B. Silcott, *Associate Director*
William L. Allen, William R. Gray, *Assistant Directors*

BOOKS FOR WORLD EXPLORERS

Ralph Gray, *Editor*
Pat Robbins, *Managing Editor*
Ursula Perrin Vosseler, *Art Director*

STAFF FOR *MORE FAR-OUT FACTS*:

Pat Robbins, *Managing Editor*
Glover S. Johns III, *Picture Editor*
Drayton Hawkins, *Designer*
Roger B. Hirschland, Jane R. McGoldrick, *Assistant Text Editors*
Joanna Biggar, Jan Leslie Cook, Jacqueline Geschickter, Kathleen Gibbons, Michael Lipske, Theresa K. McFadden, Wendy Miller, Catherine O'Neill, Elizabeth L. Parker, Edith K. Pendleton, Scott Rhodes, *Writers*
Tee Loftin, *Researcher and Assistant to the Managing Editor*
Gloria LaFay, *Researcher*
Kathryn P. Ingraham, *Research Assistant*
Nancy J. Harvey, *Editorial Assistant*
Artemis S. Lampathakis, *Illustrations Assistant*
Mary Jane Gore, *Art Secretary*
John D. Garst, Jr., *Map Production*

***FAR-OUT FUN!* BOOKLET:**

Patricia N. Holland, *Project Editor;* Ross Bankson, *Text Editor;* Drayton Hawkins, *Designer;* Peter J. Balch, Art Iddings, Roz Schanzer, *Artists*

ENGRAVING, PRINTING, AND PRODUCT MANUFACTURE:

Robert W. Messer, *Manager;* George V. White, *Production Manager;* Mark R. Dunlevy, *Production Project Manager;* Richard A. McClure, Raja D. Murshed, David V. Showers, Gregory Storer, *Assistant Production Managers;* Katherine H. Donohue, *Senior Production Assistant;* Mary A. Bennett, *Production Assistant;* Katherine R. Leitch, *Production Staff Assistant*

STAFF ASSISTANTS: Nancy F. Berry, Pamela A. Black, Nettie Burke, Mary Elizabeth Davis, Claire M. Doig, Rosamund Garner, Victoria D. Garrett, Jane R. Halpin, Sheryl A. Hoey, Joan Hurst, Virginia W. McCoy, Merrick P. Murdock, Cleo Petroff, Victoria I. Piscopo, Tammy Presley, Carol A. Rocheleau, Katheryn M. Slocum, Jenny Takacs, Carole L. Tyler

MARKET RESEARCH: Marjorie E. Hofman, Carrla L. Holmes, Meg McElligott Kieffer, Stephen F. Moss, Susan D. Snell

INDEX: George I. Burneston III

Composition for MORE FAR-OUT FACTS by National Geographic's Photographic Services, Carl M. Shrader, Chief; Lawrence F. Ludwig, Assistant Chief. Printed and bound by Holladay-Tyler Printing Corp., Rockville, Md. Color separations by the Lanman-Progressive Co., Washington, D. C.; Lincoln Graphics, Inc., Cherry Hill, N.J.; NEC, Inc., Nashville, Tenn. FAR-OUT FUN! printed by Federated Lithographers and Printers, Inc., Providence, R.I.; *Classroom Activities Folder* produced by Mazer Corporation, Dayton, Ohio.